The Natural Healing Handbook: A Guide to Effective Remedies for Common Ailments

BY

MUBARAK ALI

DISCLAIMER

The information provided in this book, "The Natural Healing Handbook: A Guide to Effective Remedies for Common Ailments", is for educational purposes only and is not intended as medical advice. The author and publisher of this book are not responsible for any adverse effects or consequences resulting from the use of the suggestions, recommendations, or procedures described in this book.

It is important to note that this book is not a substitute for medical advice, diagnosis, or treatment. While the remedies described in this book are natural and effective for many people, they are not a guaranteed cure for any particular ailment, and individual results may vary.

Furthermore, it is important to consult with a healthcare professional before using any remedies described in this book, particularly if you have a pre-existing medical condition or are taking any medications. This book should not be used to replace prescribed medication or other medical treatments, and it is not intended to diagnose or treat any medical condition.

Introduction

Welcome to The Natural Healing Handbook, a comprehensive guide to effective remedies for common ailments. This book is designed to provide you with valuable information on natural healing methods that can be used to treat a wide range of health conditions.

In today's fast-paced world, we often turn to prescription drugs or over-the-counter medications to quickly alleviate our symptoms. However, many of these treatments can come with unwanted side effects and fail to address the root cause of the issue. Natural healing remedies, on the other hand, focus on promoting overall health and well-being, rather than just symptom relief.

Whether you are new to natural healing or have already incorporated it into your life, this handbook will provide you with valuable insights and tips to help you achieve optimal health and wellness. So, grab a cup of tea, get cozy, and let's explore the world of natural healing together.

Getting started

Understanding the principles of natural healing

Natural healing is the practice of using non-invasive and non-toxic methods to treat various health conditions. This approach to healing is based on the understanding that the body has an innate ability to heal itself. The principles of natural healing involve addressing the root cause of the problem, restoring balance to the body, and promoting optimal health and wellness. In this chapter, we will explore the principles of natural healing in detail.

The Body's Innate Healing Ability

The human body is a complex system that has the ability to heal itself. The body has an innate ability to repair damaged tissue, fight off infections, and maintain a state of balance or homeostasis. Natural healing principles focus on supporting the body's own healing ability, rather than suppressing symptoms with medication.

Addressing the Root Cause of the Problem

The principles of natural healing emphasize the importance of addressing the root cause of a health problem, rather than just treating the symptoms. This means that practitioners of natural healing will often spend a significant amount of time with their patients, gathering information about their health history, lifestyle, and environmental factors that may be contributing to their condition. By identifying the underlying cause of the problem, natural healers can develop an effective treatment plan that will promote long-term healing.

Restoring Balance to the Body

The principles of natural healing recognize the importance of restoring balance to the body. This means addressing imbalances in the physical, mental, and emotional aspects of the individual. Natural healers will often use a combination of therapies, including nutrition, herbal medicine, acupuncture, massage, and meditation to help restore balance to the body.

The Importance of Prevention

Natural healing principles emphasize the importance of prevention as a key component of maintaining optimal health. This means taking steps to maintain a healthy lifestyle, including eating a nutritious diet, getting regular exercise, managing stress, and getting enough sleep. By focusing on prevention, individuals can reduce their risk of developing health problems in the future.

The Mind-Body Connection

The principles of natural healing recognize the important connection between the mind and the body. This means that mental and emotional factors can play a significant role in physical health. Natural healers will often work with their patients to address stress, anxiety, depression, and other emotional issues that may be impacting their physical health.

Individualized Treatment

Natural healing principles emphasize the importance of individualized treatment. This means that practitioners of natural healing will develop a treatment plan that is tailored to the unique needs of each patient. This may involve using a combination of therapies, including nutrition, herbal medicine, acupuncture, massage, and other modalities.

The Role of Nutrition

The principles of natural healing recognize the important role that nutrition plays in promoting optimal health. Natural healers will often focus on using whole foods and supplements to provide the body with the nutrients it needs to function properly. This may involve recommending specific foods or supplements to address deficiencies or imbalances in the body.

Natural healing principles also recognize the importance of working with other healthcare providers to promote optimal health. This may include working with a physician or other healthcare provider to coordinate care and ensure that the patient receives the best possible treatment.

In addition to addressing physical health, natural healing principles also recognize the importance of emotional and mental health. Natural healers will often work with their patients to address stress, anxiety, and other emotional issues that may be impacting their physical health. This may involve using techniques such as meditation, yoga, or other mind-body practices.

Overall, the principles of natural healing offer a holistic approach to health and wellness. By addressing the root cause of health problems, restoring balance to the body, and promoting prevention, natural healing practitioners can help individuals achieve optimal health and wellbeing. Whether it's using nutrition, herbal medicine, acupuncture, massage, or other modalities, natural healing offers a safe and effective way to promote healing and wellbeing.

The benefits of natural remedies over conventional medicine

The use of natural remedies to treat common ailments has been around for centuries, long before modern medicine emerged. Natural remedies can be anything from herbs, spices, fruits, vegetables, and other natural substances. In this chapter, we will explore the benefits of natural remedies over conventional medicine and how they can effectively treat common ailments.

Natural remedies are safer

One of the primary benefits of natural remedies over conventional medicine is their safety. Natural remedies are derived from plants, herbs, and other natural substances, and do not contain any artificial chemicals or additives. This means they are much less likely to cause harmful side effects or other adverse reactions.

On the other hand, conventional medicines are often made from synthetic compounds that can have a range of side effects, some of which can be severe. These side effects can include allergic reactions, gastrointestinal problems, and even organ damage. In contrast, natural remedies are generally considered safe and are less likely to cause harm.

Natural remedies are cost-effective

Another benefit of natural remedies is that they are often much cheaper than conventional medicines. Most natural remedies can be found at health food stores, online, or even in your own backyard. This makes them an excellent option for people who are on a tight budget or do not have access to traditional medical care.

In contrast, conventional medicines can be expensive, especially if they are not covered by insurance. This can make it difficult for some people to afford the treatment they need, and can even lead to them avoiding medical care altogether.

Natural remedies are effective

While conventional medicine is often considered the gold standard for treating many health conditions, natural remedies can also be highly effective. In fact, many natural remedies have been used for centuries to treat a variety of ailments, and modern research has confirmed their effectiveness.

For example, ginger has been used for centuries to treat nausea and vomiting, and research has shown that it can be as effective as conventional anti-nausea medications. Similarly, chamomile has been used for centuries to treat anxiety and insomnia, and recent studies have shown that it can be as effective as some prescription medications.

Natural remedies can help prevent disease

Natural remedies can also be effective in preventing disease. Many natural remedies contain antioxidants and other nutrients that can help boost the immune system and protect the body from harmful pathogens.

For example, garlic is known for its ability to boost the immune system and fight off infections. Similarly, echinacea has been shown to stimulate the immune system and reduce the risk of catching a cold or flu.

Natural remedies are often more sustainable

Finally, natural remedies are often more sustainable than conventional medicines. Many conventional medicines are made from synthetic compounds that are derived from non-renewable resources and can be harmful to the environment.

In contrast, natural remedies are often derived from renewable resources, such as plants and herbs, and are often grown using organic and sustainable farming practices. This makes them a more environmentally friendly option for people who are concerned about the impact their healthcare choices have on the planet.

Additionally, natural remedies can offer a more personalized approach to healthcare. Every individual's body is unique, and natural remedies can be customized to meet individual needs. For example, some people may have allergies or sensitivities to certain medications, but natural remedies can often be tailored to work around these limitations.

Moreover, natural remedies can offer a holistic approach to healthcare. Rather than simply treating the symptoms of a specific ailment, natural remedies can work to support the body's overall health and wellbeing. For instance, some natural remedies can promote healthy digestion, reduce inflammation, and improve mood, which can all have a positive impact on a person's overall health.

It is important to note that natural remedies are not always the best option for every health condition. In some cases, conventional medicine may be necessary, particularly for serious or life-threatening illnesses. However, natural remedies can be an effective and safe alternative for many common ailments, particularly when used in conjunction with conventional treatments.

In conclusion, natural remedies offer numerous benefits over conventional medicine. They are safer, more cost-effective, effective, and can help prevent disease while being more sustainable. Natural remedies also offer a more personalized and holistic approach to healthcare. By incorporating natural remedies into their healthcare routine, individuals can improve their overall health and wellbeing while minimizing their environmental impact.

How to integrate natural remedies into your lifestyle

Natural remedies have been used for centuries to treat common ailments and promote overall health and wellbeing. In recent years, there has been a renewed interest in natural remedies as people seek alternatives to conventional medicine. This chapter will provide a detailed guide on how to integrate natural remedies into your lifestyle, including tips on how to choose the right remedies, how to use them safely and effectively, and how to make them a part of your daily routine.

Choosing the Right Natural Remedies

The first step in integrating natural remedies into your lifestyle is to choose the right remedies for your specific needs. There are a wide variety of natural remedies available, each with its own unique properties and benefits. Some of the most common natural remedies include herbal supplements, essential oils, homeopathic remedies, and traditional Chinese medicine.

When choosing natural remedies, it is important to do your research and consult with a healthcare professional if necessary. Some natural remedies can interact with prescription medications, and others may not be appropriate for certain medical conditions.

It is also important to choose high-quality natural remedies from reputable sources. Look for products that are certified organic, non-GMO, and free from harmful additives and preservatives. Read reviews and testimonials from other users to get an idea of the effectiveness and safety of the products you are considering.

Using Natural Remedies Safely and Effectively

Once you have chosen the natural remedies that are right for you, it is important to use them safely and effectively. Some natural remedies can be powerful and may cause side effects if not used properly. Always follow the recommended dosage and usage instructions provided with your natural remedies, and do not exceed the recommended amount.

It is also important to use natural remedies consistently in order to see results. Some remedies may take longer to work than others, so be patient and stick with them. Keep a journal to track your progress and note any changes in your symptoms or overall health.

In addition to using natural remedies as directed, it is also important to make lifestyle changes that support your health and wellbeing. This includes eating a healthy diet, getting regular exercise, getting enough sleep, and managing stress. Natural remedies can be a valuable tool in promoting health and healing, but they are not a substitute for a healthy lifestyle.

Making Natural Remedies a Part of Your Daily Routine

Finally, in order to truly integrate natural remedies into your lifestyle, it is important to make them a part of your daily routine. This means incorporating them into your daily habits and rituals, such as your morning routine or bedtime routine.

For example, you might start your day with a cup of herbal tea or a smoothie made with natural supplements. You might use essential oils to create a relaxing atmosphere in your home or office, or to promote better sleep at night. You might take a homeopathic remedy before bed to help with insomnia or anxiety.

Whatever natural remedies you choose, find ways to incorporate them into your daily life in a way that feels natural and sustainable. This will help you to reap the full benefits of natural healing and promote overall health and wellbeing over the long term.

Incorporating Natural Remedies into Your Diet

One of the easiest ways to integrate natural remedies into your lifestyle is by incorporating them into your diet. There are many natural remedies that can be added to your meals or taken as supplements to provide a range of health benefits.

Some of the most common natural remedies that can be incorporated into your diet include:

Turmeric:

Turmeric is a spice that is commonly used in Indian and Middle Eastern cuisine. It contains a compound called curcumin, which has powerful anti-inflammatory properties and has been shown to improve brain function and reduce the risk of chronic diseases such as heart disease and cancer.

Ginger:

Ginger is a root that is commonly used in Asian cuisine. It has been shown to have anti-inflammatory and antioxidant properties and can help to relieve nausea, pain, and menstrual cramps.

Garlic:

Garlic is a bulb that is commonly used in Mediterranean cuisine. It contains compounds that can help to lower cholesterol levels, improve blood pressure, and boost the immune system.

Green tea:

Green tea is a type of tea that is rich in antioxidants and other compounds that can help to reduce the risk of chronic diseases such as heart disease, diabetes, and cancer.

Omega-3 fatty acids:

Omega-3 fatty acids are a type of healthy fat that is found in fatty fish, nuts, and seeds. They have been shown to reduce inflammation, improve brain function, and lower the risk of heart disease and other chronic diseases.

When incorporating natural remedies into your diet, it is important to choose high-quality ingredients and to prepare them in a way that preserves their health benefits. For example, turmeric is best consumed with black pepper, which can enhance the absorption of curcumin in the body. Garlic is most effective when consumed raw or lightly cooked, as cooking can reduce its health benefits.

In addition to adding natural remedies to your diet, you can also take natural supplements to provide additional support for your health and wellbeing. Some of the most common natural supplements include:

Vitamin D:

Vitamin D is essential for bone health and immune function. It is found in fatty fish, egg yolks, and fortified foods, but many people do not get enough from their diet alone.

Magnesium:

Magnesium is a mineral that is essential for over 300 biochemical reactions in the body. It can help to reduce stress and anxiety, improve sleep, and reduce muscle cramps and spasms.

Probiotics:

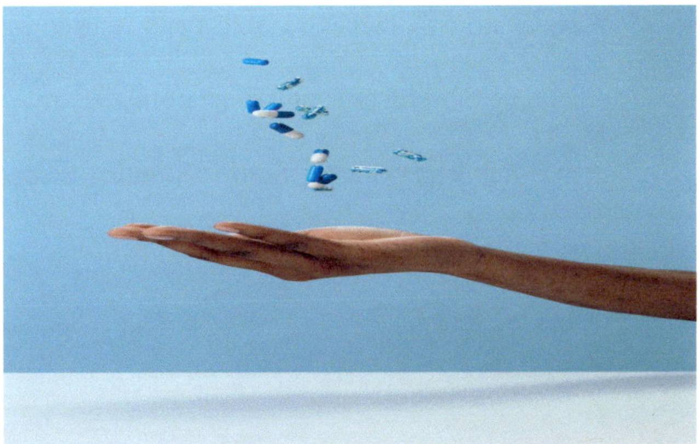

Probiotics are beneficial bacteria that live in the gut. They can help to improve digestion, boost the immune system, and reduce inflammation.

Adaptogens: Adaptogens are natural substances that can help the body to adapt to stress and promote balance and resilience. Some common adaptogens include ashwagandha, rhodiola, and holy basil.

Integrating Natural Remedies into Your Daily Routine

In addition to incorporating natural remedies into your diet, there are many other ways to integrate them into your daily routine. Some of the most common methods include:

Essential oils: Essential oils are highly concentrated plant extracts that can be used for a range of purposes, including aromatherapy, massage, and skincare. Some common essential oils include lavender, peppermint, and tea tree.

Herbal teas: Herbal teas are a great way to enjoy the health benefits of herbs and other natural ingredients. Some common herbal teas include chamomile, ginger, and echinacea.

Homeopathic remedies: Homeopathic remedies are highly diluted substances that are used to stimulate the body's natural healing processes. They can be taken orally or applied topically to treat a range of conditions.

Traditional Chinese medicine: Traditional Chinese medicine is a holistic system of medicine that includes acupuncture, herbal medicine, and other modalities. It can be used to treat a wide range of conditions, from pain and inflammation to digestive issues and infertility.

When integrating natural remedies into your daily routine, it is important to start slowly and gradually build up your use of these remedies. This will give your body time to adjust and ensure that you are not experiencing any adverse reactions.

Here are some tips for integrating natural remedies into your daily routine:

Start with one or two remedies that you are interested in trying. Research them thoroughly and consult with a healthcare professional if necessary.

Make a plan for how you will incorporate these remedies into your daily routine. For example, you might use an essential oil diffuser in your bedroom at night, or drink a cup of herbal tea after dinner.

Be consistent with your use of natural remedies. It can take time to see results, so give yourself at least a few weeks to assess the effectiveness of the remedies you are using.

Keep a journal to track your progress and note any changes in your symptoms or overall health. This can help you to identify which remedies are most effective for you and make adjustments to your routine as needed.

Be open to trying new remedies and adjusting your routine as your needs change. Natural remedies can be a powerful tool for promoting health and healing, but they may not work for everyone or in every situation.

Conclusion

Integrating natural remedies into your lifestyle can be a powerful way to promote health and healing, and to support overall wellbeing. By choosing the right remedies, using them safely and effectively, and making them a part of your daily routine, you can harness the power of natural healing and transform your health and vitality. Remember to do your research, consult with a healthcare professional if necessary, and make lifestyle changes that support your overall health and wellbeing. With time and consistency, natural remedies can become a valuable tool in your journey to optimal health and vitality.

Building Your Natural Healing Toolkit

Essential oils and their uses

Essential oils are concentrated plant extracts that are used for a variety of purposes, including aromatherapy, massage, and natural healing remedies. They are derived from different parts of plants, including flowers, leaves, stems, roots, and seeds, through a process of steam distillation, cold pressing, or solvent extraction.

Essential oils are highly aromatic and have powerful therapeutic properties that can benefit both the mind and body. They are composed of a complex mixture of volatile organic compounds, including terpenes, phenols, ketones, aldehydes, and esters, which give them their distinctive fragrance and therapeutic effects.

In this chapter, we will explore the history, science, and safety of essential oils, as well as their different types and applications.

Section 1.1: History of Essential Oils

Essential oils have been used for thousands of years for their medicinal and cosmetic properties. The ancient Egyptians were known to use aromatic oils for embalming, healing, and perfuming, while the Greeks and Romans used them for medicinal purposes, such as treating wounds and infections.

In the Middle Ages, essential oils were used to mask unpleasant odors and to prevent the spread of disease during the plague. They were also used in perfumes and cosmetics by the wealthy elite.

During the Renaissance, the use of essential oils became more widespread, with the development of distillation techniques that allowed for the extraction of essential oils from a wider range of plants. In the 19th century, essential oils were used extensively in medicine, particularly in France, where they were used to treat a variety of conditions, such as cholera and tuberculosis.

Today, essential oils are widely used for aromatherapy, massage, and natural healing remedies. They are also used in perfumes, cosmetics, and household products, such as cleaning agents and air fresheners.

Section 1.2: Science of Essential Oils

The therapeutic properties of essential oils are due to their chemical composition, which varies depending on the plant from which they are derived. Each essential oil contains a unique combination of volatile organic compounds, which can have different effects on the body.

For example, lavender oil contains linalool and linalyl acetate, which have sedative and calming effects, while peppermint oil contains menthol and menthone, which have analgesic and anti-inflammatory effects.

When inhaled or applied topically, essential oils can interact with the limbic system in the brain, which is responsible for regulating emotions, memory, and behavior. They can also penetrate the skin and enter the bloodstream, where they can have systemic effects on the body.

Research has shown that essential oils can have a range of therapeutic effects, such as reducing stress and anxiety, improving sleep, relieving pain and inflammation, and boosting the immune system. However, more research is needed to fully understand their mechanisms of action and potential benefits.

Section 1.3: Safety of Essential Oils

Although essential oils are natural products, they can be potent and potentially harmful if used improperly. It is important to use essential oils safely and to be aware of any potential side effects or interactions.

Some essential oils, such as peppermint and eucalyptus, can be irritating or even toxic if ingested or applied directly to the skin at high concentrations. Others, such as citrus oils, can cause photosensitivity or skin irritation when exposed to sunlight.

Essential oils should be diluted in a carrier oil, such as coconut or jojoba oil, before being applied to the skin. The recommended dilution rate is typically 1-3% for adults and 0.5-1% for children and the elderly.

It is also important to be aware of any potential drug interactions when using essential oils.
Some essential oils can interact with certain medications, such as blood thinners and antidepressants, and may increase or decrease their effectiveness. It is recommended to consult with a healthcare professional before using essential oils if you are taking any medications.

In addition, pregnant women and individuals with certain medical conditions, such as epilepsy or asthma, should use caution when using essential oils and should consult with a healthcare professional before use.

Section 1.4: Types of Essential Oils

There are hundreds of different types of essential oils, each with its own unique aroma and therapeutic properties. Here are some of the most popular essential oils and their uses:

Lavender: Calming and relaxing, promotes sleep, relieves anxiety and stress, soothes skin irritations, and promotes wound healing.

Peppermint: Stimulating and invigorating, relieves headaches and nausea, soothes sore muscles, and improves digestion.

Tea tree: Antimicrobial and anti-inflammatory, treats acne, soothes skin irritations, and promotes wound healing.

Eucalyptus: Respiratory and immune support, relieves congestion and coughs, soothes sore muscles, and repels insects.

Lemon: Cleansing and uplifting, improves mood, boosts immunity, and freshens the air.

Rosemary: Mental and physical stimulation, improves memory and concentration, promotes hair growth, and relieves pain and inflammation.

Frankincense: Relaxing and grounding, promotes spiritual and emotional balance, reduces inflammation and pain, and supports immunity.

Chamomile: Calming and soothing, promotes relaxation and sleep, soothes skin irritations, and relieves digestive issues.

These are just a few examples of the many essential oils available, each with its own unique benefits and uses.

Section 1.5: Applications of Essential Oils

Essential oils can be used in a variety of ways, depending on the desired effect and personal preference. Here are some of the most common applications:

Aromatherapy: Essential oils can be diffused into the air using a diffuser or added to a bath to promote relaxation, improve mood, and reduce stress and anxiety.

Massage: Essential oils can be diluted in a carrier oil and used for massage to relieve muscle tension, promote relaxation, and improve circulation.

Topical application: Essential oils can be diluted in a carrier oil and applied to the skin for a variety of purposes, such as treating skin irritations, relieving pain and inflammation, and promoting wound healing.

Inhalation: Essential oils can be inhaled directly from the bottle or added to a bowl of hot water for respiratory support and to relieve congestion and coughs.

Household use: Essential oils can be added to cleaning agents and air fresheners to create a natural and non-toxic environment.

Overall, essential oils are versatile and powerful natural remedies that can be used for a variety of purposes. However, it is important to use them safely and to be aware of any potential side effects or interactions. With proper use, essential oils can be a safe and effective alternative to conventional treatments for common ailments.

Herbal remedies and their benefits

Herbal remedies have been used for thousands of years to treat a variety of ailments. These natural remedies have gained popularity in recent years due to their effectiveness and lack of side effects. In this chapter, we will explore some of the most popular herbal remedies and their benefits.

Echinacea

Echinacea is a popular herbal remedy that is known for its immune-boosting properties. It has been used for centuries to treat a variety of ailments, including colds, flu, and infections. Echinacea can also help reduce inflammation, which makes it an effective remedy for arthritis and other inflammatory conditions.

Ginger

Ginger is a common spice that is used in many cuisines around the world. It is also a popular herbal remedy that has been used for centuries to treat nausea, vomiting, and other digestive issues. Ginger can also help reduce inflammation and pain, making it an effective remedy for arthritis and other inflammatory conditions.

Turmeric

Turmeric is a spice that is commonly used in Indian and Middle Eastern cuisine. It is also a popular herbal remedy that is known for its anti-inflammatory and antioxidant properties. Turmeric can help reduce inflammation and pain, making it an effective remedy for arthritis and other inflammatory conditions.

Chamomile

Chamomile is a popular herbal remedy that is known for its calming and soothing properties. It is commonly used to treat anxiety, insomnia, and other sleep disorders. Chamomile can also help reduce inflammation, making it an effective remedy for skin conditions like eczema and psoriasis.

Peppermint

Peppermint is a popular herb that is commonly used to flavor food and drinks. It is also a popular herbal remedy that is known for its digestive properties. Peppermint can help soothe upset stomachs, reduce gas and bloating, and relieve nausea.

Valerian

Valerian is a popular herbal remedy that is known for its calming and sedative properties. It is commonly used to treat anxiety, insomnia, and other sleep disorders. Valerian can also help reduce muscle tension and pain, making it an effective remedy for conditions like migraines and tension headaches.

Milk Thistle

Milk thistle is a popular herbal remedy that is known for its liver-protective properties. It is commonly used to treat liver diseases like cirrhosis and hepatitis. Milk thistle can also help reduce inflammation and oxidative stress, making it an effective remedy for conditions like diabetes and heart disease.

St. John's Wort

St. John's Wort is a popular herbal remedy that is known for its antidepressant properties. It is commonly used to treat mild to moderate depression. St. John's Wort can also help reduce anxiety and improve sleep quality.

Ginkgo Biloba

Ginkgo Biloba is a popular herbal remedy that is known for its cognitive-enhancing properties. It is commonly used to improve memory, concentration, and overall cognitive function. Ginkgo Biloba can also help reduce inflammation and oxidative stress, making it an effective remedy for conditions like Alzheimer's and Parkinson's disease.

Saw Palmetto

Saw Palmetto is a popular herbal remedy that is known for its prostate-protective properties. It is commonly used to treat benign prostatic hyperplasia (BPH), a condition that affects the prostate gland in men. Saw Palmetto can also help reduce inflammation and oxidative stress, making it an effective remedy for conditions like acne and hair loss.

Conclusion

Herbal remedies have been used for thousands of years to treat a variety of ailments. These natural remedies have gained popularity in recent years due to their effectiveness and lack of side effects. Echinacea, ginger, turmeric , chamomile, peppermint, valerian, milk thistle, St. John's Wort, ginkgo biloba, and saw palmetto are just a few examples of popular herbal remedies and their benefits. While herbal remedies can be effective, it's important to note that they should not be used as a replacement for traditional medical treatments. It's always best to consult with a healthcare professional before trying any new herbal remedy, especially if you have an existing medical condition or are taking medications.

In addition to consulting with a healthcare professional, it's also important to purchase high-quality herbal remedies from reputable sources. Many herbal remedies are not regulated by the FDA, so it's important to do your research and ensure that you're purchasing products that are safe and effective. Look for products that have been third-party tested and certified, and avoid products that contain additives or fillers.

Overall, herbal remedies can be a valuable addition to your health and wellness routine. Whether you're looking to boost your immune system, soothe digestive issues, or improve cognitive function, there's likely an herbal remedy that can help. Just remember to use caution, do your research, and always consult with a healthcare professional before trying any new remedies.

Homeopathic remedies and how they work

Homeopathy is a form of alternative medicine that was developed in the late 18th century by German physician Samuel Hahnemann. Homeopathy is based on the principle of "like cures like," which means that a substance that causes symptoms in a healthy person can be used to treat similar symptoms in a sick person. Homeopathic remedies are made from natural substances such as plants, minerals, and animal products, which are diluted and succussed (shaken) to increase their potency.

In this chapter, we will explore the principles behind homeopathic remedies, how they are made, and how they work to treat common ailments.

Principles of Homeopathic Remedies

The principles of homeopathic remedies are based on two main concepts: the Law of Similars and the Law of Minimum Dose.

The Law of Similars states that a substance that causes symptoms in a healthy person can be used to treat similar symptoms in a sick person. This concept is based on the idea that the body has the ability to heal itself, and that by introducing a small amount of a substance that causes similar symptoms, the body will be stimulated to heal itself.

The Law of Minimum Dose states that the smaller the dose of a substance, the more effective it will be in treating a condition. This concept is based on the idea that the body has an innate intelligence that can recognize and respond to small amounts of a substance.

How Homeopathic Remedies are Made

Homeopathic remedies are made from natural substances such as plants, minerals, and animal products. The substance is first diluted in a solution such as water or alcohol, and then successed (shaken) to increase its potency.

The dilution process involves a series of steps, each of which involves diluting the original substance with water or alcohol. The most common dilution ratios used in homeopathy are 1:10 (also known as a 1X dilution), 1:100 (a 2X dilution), and 1:1000 (a 3X dilution).

After each dilution step, the solution is successed (shaken) vigorously. This process is thought to release the energy of the original substance into the solution, making it more potent.

The dilution and succussion process is repeated several times until the desired potency is reached. Homeopathic remedies are usually labeled with a number and letter designation, which indicate the dilution level and the type of remedy.

How Homeopathic Remedies Work

The exact mechanism by which homeopathic remedies work is not fully understood, but there are several theories.

One theory is that homeopathic remedies work by stimulating the body's innate healing response. The small amounts of the active substance in the remedy are thought to stimulate the body's immune system and activate its healing mechanisms.

Another theory is that homeopathic remedies work by influencing the body's energy fields. It is thought that the succussion process releases the energy of the original substance into the solution, creating an energetic imprint that can influence the body's energy fields and promote healing.

Homeopathic remedies are also thought to work on a psychological level. The act of taking a remedy and the belief that it will help can have a powerful placebo effect, which can influence the body's healing response.

Common Homeopathic Remedies and Their Uses

There are hundreds of homeopathic remedies available, each with their own specific uses and indications. Here are some of the most commonly used remedies and their uses:

Arnica: used for pain, swelling, and bruising

Belladonna: used for fever, sore throat, and ear infections

Calendula: used for skin irritation, cuts, and wounds

Chamomilla: used for teething pain in infants, colic, and irritability

Nux vomica: used for digestive issues such as constipation, indigestion, and nausea

Pulsatilla: used for respiratory issues such as colds, coughs, and allergies

Rhus tox: used for joint pain, stiffness, and rheumatism

Sulphur: used for skin conditions such as eczema, psoriasis, and acne

These remedies can be taken in various forms, including tablets, pellets, liquid drops, and creams. They are typically available over-the-counter at health food stores and pharmacies.

Homeopathic remedies can be used to treat a wide range of acute and chronic conditions, including colds, flu, allergies, asthma, arthritis, anxiety, depression, and more.

Potential Benefits and Risks of Homeopathic Remedies

One of the main benefits of homeopathic remedies is that they are safe and non-toxic. Because they are made from natural substances and are highly diluted, they have no side effects or interactions with other medications.

Homeopathic remedies are also relatively inexpensive and easy to use. They can be taken at home without the need for a prescription or medical supervision.

However, homeopathy is a controversial field, and many medical professionals are skeptical of its efficacy. There is limited scientific evidence to support the effectiveness of homeopathic remedies, and some studies have found that they are no more effective than a placebo.

Additionally, because homeopathic remedies are highly diluted, they may not contain enough of the active substance to be effective. This has led some critics to question whether homeopathy is a valid form of medicine.

Conclusion

Homeopathic remedies are a form of alternative medicine that are based on the principles of "like cures like" and the Law of Minimum Dose. They are made from natural substances and are highly diluted and succussed to increase their potency.

While the exact mechanism by which homeopathic remedies work is not fully understood, they are thought to stimulate the body's innate healing response, influence the body's energy fields, and have a psychological effect.

Homeopathic remedies can be used to treat a wide range of acute and chronic conditions, but their efficacy is controversial, and there is limited scientific evidence to support their effectiveness.

Overall, homeopathic remedies can be a safe and non-toxic alternative to conventional medicine for some people, but it is important to consult with a healthcare provider before using them to treat a serious condition.

Vitamins, minerals, and supplements for natural healing

The use of vitamins, minerals, and supplements for natural healing is becoming increasingly popular as people look for alternative ways to maintain their health and treat common ailments. This chapter will provide an overview of these nutrients and their roles in the body, as well as the benefits of using them for natural healing.

1.1 What are Vitamins, Minerals, and Supplements?

Vitamins are organic compounds that the body needs in small amounts to maintain good health and prevent disease. There are 13 essential vitamins, including vitamins A, C, D, E, K, and the B vitamins.

Minerals are inorganic substances that the body needs in small amounts for various functions, such as building strong bones and teeth, producing hormones, and maintaining a healthy heartbeat. There are two types of minerals: macrominerals, which are needed in larger amounts, and trace minerals, which are needed in smaller amounts.

Supplements are products that contain vitamins, minerals, or other nutrients, such as herbs or amino acids, that are taken orally to supplement the diet. They are available in various forms, including capsules, tablets, liquids, and powders.

1.2 Roles of Vitamins, Minerals, and Supplements in the Body

Vitamins, minerals, and supplements play crucial roles in many bodily functions. Here are some examples:

Vitamin A: Helps maintain healthy skin, eyes, and immune system function.

Vitamin C: Helps the body produce collagen, a protein that supports skin, bones, and blood vessels, and boosts immune system function.

Vitamin D: Helps the body absorb calcium, which is needed for strong bones and teeth, and supports immune system function.

Vitamin E: Acts as an antioxidant, protecting cells from damage caused by free radicals.

Vitamin K: Plays a role in blood clotting and bone health.

B vitamins: Help the body produce energy from food, support brain function, and maintain healthy skin, hair, and nails.

Calcium: Builds and maintains strong bones and teeth, and helps muscles and nerves function properly.

Iron: Helps the body produce red blood cells, which carry oxygen throughout the body.

Magnesium: Helps muscles and nerves function properly, regulates heart rhythm, and supports immune system function.

Zinc: Supports immune system function and helps the body produce DNA and proteins.

1.3 Benefits of Using Vitamins, Minerals, and Supplements for Natural Healing

Using vitamins, minerals, and supplements for natural healing can have several benefits:

They can help fill nutrient gaps in the diet: Many people do not get enough essential vitamins and minerals from their diet alone. Taking supplements can help ensure that the body has all the nutrients it needs to function properly.

They can support immune system function: Many vitamins and minerals, such as vitamin C, vitamin D, and zinc, play important roles in immune system function. Taking supplements containing these nutrients can help support a healthy immune system.

They can help manage symptoms of certain conditions: Some supplements, such as omega-3 fatty acids and magnesium, have been shown to help reduce inflammation and alleviate symptoms of conditions such as arthritis and migraines.

They can promote overall health and well-being: Taking supplements can help support various bodily functions, such as energy production, skin health, and heart health, promoting overall health and well-being.

Chapter 2: Vitamins for Natural Healing

This chapter will focus on the essential vitamins and their roles in natural healing, as well as the benefits of taking vitamin supplements.

2.1 Vitamin A

Vitamin A is an essential vitamin that is important for maintaining healthy skin, eyes, and immune system function. It is found in many foods, including liver, eggs, milk, and dark leafy vegetables like spinach and kale. Vitamin A supplements are also available in various forms, including capsules and tablets.

2.1.1 Roles in Natural Healing

Vitamin A plays several roles in natural healing:

Skin health: Vitamin A is important for maintaining healthy skin, as it helps to prevent dryness, flakiness, and wrinkles. It also supports wound healing and reduces the risk of skin infections.
Eye health: Vitamin A is crucial for maintaining good vision, as it helps to prevent night blindness and other vision problems.
Immune system function: Vitamin A plays a key role in immune system function, helping to protect the body from infections and diseases.

2.1.2 Benefits of Taking Vitamin A Supplements

Taking vitamin A supplements can have several benefits for natural healing:

Improved skin health: Vitamin A supplements can help improve the appearance and texture of the skin, reducing dryness, flakiness, and wrinkles.
Better vision: Vitamin A supplements can help prevent vision problems, such as night blindness and age-related macular degeneration.
Enhanced immune system function: Vitamin A supplements can help support immune system function, reducing the risk of infections and diseases.

2.2 Vitamin C

Vitamin C, also known as ascorbic acid, is an essential vitamin that is important for collagen production, wound healing, and immune system function. It is found in many fruits and vegetables, including citrus fruits, berries, peppers, and broccoli. Vitamin C supplements are also available in various forms, including capsules, tablets, and powders.

2.2.1 Roles in Natural Healing

Vitamin C plays several roles in natural healing:

Collagen production: Vitamin C is essential for collagen production, a protein that supports skin, bones, and blood vessels.
Wound healing: Vitamin C helps the body produce new tissue, including skin, blood vessels, and bones, which is crucial for wound healing.
Immune system function: Vitamin C supports immune system function, helping to protect the body from infections and diseases.

2.2.2 Benefits of Taking Vitamin C Supplements

Taking vitamin C supplements can have several benefits for natural healing:

Improved skin health: Vitamin C supplements can help improve the appearance and texture of the skin, reducing the signs of aging and promoting a healthy glow.
Faster wound healing: Vitamin C supplements can help speed up the healing process of wounds and injuries.
Enhanced immune system function: Vitamin C supplements can help support immune system function, reducing the risk of infections and diseases.

2.3 Vitamin D

Vitamin D is an essential vitamin that is important for bone health, immune system function, and overall health and well-being. It is found in few foods, including fatty fish, egg yolks, and fortified milk and cereals. The body can also produce vitamin D when the skin is exposed to sunlight. Vitamin D supplements are also available in various forms, including capsules and tablets.

2.3.1 Roles in Natural Healing

Vitamin D plays several roles in natural healing:

Bone health: Vitamin D is essential for strong bones and teeth, as it helps the body absorb calcium and phosphorus.

Immune system function: Vitamin D supports immune system function, helping to protect the body from infections and diseases.

Overall health and well-being: Vitamin D has been linked to many health benefits, including a reduced risk of certain types of cancer, heart disease, and autoimmune disorders.

2.3.2 Benefits of Taking Vitamin D Supplements

Taking vitamin D supplements can have several benefits for natural healing:

Improved bone health: Vitamin D supplements can help prevent osteoporosis and fractures by promoting strong bones and teeth.

Enhanced immune system function: Vitamin D supplements can help support immune system function, reducing the risk of infections and diseases.

Reduced risk of certain health conditions: Vitamin D supplements have been linked to a reduced risk of certain types of cancer, heart disease, and autoimmune disorders.

2.4 Vitamin E

Vitamin E is an essential vitamin that acts as an antioxidant, protecting cells from damage caused by free radicals. It is found in many foods, including nuts, seeds, and vegetable oils. Vitamin E supplements are also available in various forms, including capsules and tablets.

2.4.1 Roles in Natural Healing

Vitamin E plays several roles in natural healing:

Antioxidant: Vitamin E acts as an antioxidant, protecting cells from damage caused by free radicals, which can lead to chronic diseases and aging.

Skin health: Vitamin E helps to maintain healthy skin by reducing the signs of aging and promoting healing.

Immune system function: Vitamin E supports immune system function, helping to protect the body from infections and diseases.

2.4.2 Benefits of Taking Vitamin E Supplements

Taking vitamin E supplements can have several benefits for natural healing:

Improved skin health: Vitamin E supplements can help improve the appearance and texture of the skin, reducing the signs of aging and promoting healing.
Enhanced immune system function: Vitamin E supplements can help support immune system function, reducing the risk of infections and diseases.
Protection against chronic diseases: Vitamin E supplements may help protect against chronic diseases, such as heart disease and Alzheimer's disease, by acting as an antioxidant and reducing inflammation.

Chapter 3: Minerals for Natural Healing

This chapter will focus on the essential minerals and their roles in natural healing, as well as the benefits of taking mineral supplements.

3.1 Calcium

Calcium is an essential mineral that is important for building and maintaining strong bones and teeth, as well as supporting muscle and nerve function. It is found in many foods, including dairy products, leafy green vegetables, and fortified cereals. Calcium supplements are also available in various forms, including capsules and tablets.

3.1.1 Roles in Natural Healing

Calcium plays several roles in natural healing:

Bone and teeth health: Calcium is essential for building and maintaining strong bones and teeth.
Muscle and nerve function: Calcium helps muscles and nerves function properly, including the contraction and relaxation of muscles.
Blood clotting: Calcium plays a role in blood clotting, which is crucial for wound healing.

3.1.2 Benefits of Taking Calcium Supplements

Taking calcium supplements can have several benefits for natural healing:

Improved bone and teeth health: Calcium supplements can help prevent osteoporosis and fractures by promoting strong bones and teeth.

Enhanced muscle and nerve function: Calcium supplements can help support proper muscle and nerve function, reducing the risk of cramps and spasms.
Faster wound healing: Calcium supplements can help promote blood clotting, speeding up the healing process of wounds and injuries.

3.2 Iron

Iron is an essential mineral that is important for producing hemoglobin, a protein in red blood cells that carries oxygen throughout the body. It is found in many foods, including red meat, poultry, seafood, beans, and fortified cereals. Iron supplements are also available in various forms, including capsules and tablets.

3.2.1 Roles in Natural Healing

Iron plays several roles in natural healing:

Oxygen transport: Iron is essential for producing hemoglobin, which carries oxygen throughout the body.
Energy production: Iron is needed for the production of adenosine triphosphate (ATP), a molecule that provides energy to cells.
Immune system function: Iron supports immune system function, helping to protect the body from infections and diseases.

3.2.2 Benefits of Taking Iron Supplements

Taking iron supplements can have several benefits for natural healing:

Improved energy levels: Iron supplements can help increase energy levels by supporting ATP production.

Better oxygen transport: Iron supplements can help ensure that the body has enough hemoglobin to carry oxygen to cells, improving overall health and well-being.
Enhanced immune system function: Iron supplements can help support immune system function, reducing the risk of infections and diseases.

3.3 Magnesium

Magnesium is an essential mineral that is important for many bodily functions, including muscle and nerve function, heart health, and immune system function. It is found in many foods, including nuts, seeds, whole grains, and leafy green vegetables. Magnesium supplements are also available in various forms, including capsules and tablets.

3.3.1 Roles in Natural Healing

Magnesium plays several roles in natural healing:

Muscle and nerve function: Magnesium helps muscles and nerves function properly, regulating muscle contractions and promoting relaxation.
Heart health: Magnesium supports heart health by regulating heart rhythm and blood pressure.
Immune system function: Magnesium supports immune system function, helping to protect the body from infections and diseases.

3.3.2 Benefits of Taking Magnesium Supplements

Taking magnesium supplements can have several benefits for natural healing:

Enhanced muscle and nerve function: Magnesium supplements can help support proper muscle and nerve function, reducing the risk of cramps and spasms.
Improved heart health: Magnesium supplements can help regulate heart rhythm and blood pressure, reducing the risk of heart disease.
Enhanced immune system function: Magnesium supplements can help support immune system function, reducing the risk of infections and diseases.

3.4 Zinc

Zinc is an essential mineral that is important for many bodily functions, including immune system function, wound healing, and cell growth and division. It is found in many foods, including oysters, beef, poultry, beans, and fortified cereals. Zinc supplements are also available in various forms, including capsules and tablets.

3.4.1 Roles in Natural Healing

Zinc plays several roles in natural healing:

Immune system function: Zinc supports immune system function, helping to protect the body from infections and diseases.

Wound healing: Zinc is important for wound healing, as it helps to promote tissue growth and repair.
Cell growth and division: Zinc is necessary for cell growth and division, which is crucial for overall health and well-being.
3.4.2 Benefits of Taking Zinc Supplements

Taking zinc supplements can have several benefits for natural healing:

Enhanced immune system function: Zinc supplements can help support immune system function, reducing the risk of infections and diseases.
Faster wound healing: Zinc supplements can help promote tissue growth and repair, speeding up the healing process of wounds and injuries.
Improved overall health and well-being: Zinc supplements can help promote cell growth and division, supporting overall health and well-being.
Chapter 4: Supplements for Natural Healing

This chapter will focus on the different types of supplements, including herbs, amino acids, and probiotics, and their roles in natural healing, as well as the benefits of taking supplement combinations.

4.1 Herbs

Herbs have been used for centuries for their medicinal properties, and many are still used today for natural healing. Some common herbs used for natural healing include:

Echinacea: Used for immune system support and to reduce the symptoms of colds and flu.
St. John's wort: Used for mild to moderate depression and anxiety.
Ginkgo biloba: Used for cognitive function and to improve blood flow.
Turmeric: Used for inflammation and to reduce the risk of chronic diseases.
Garlic: Used for cardiovascular health and to support immune system function.
Herbal supplements are available in various forms, including capsules, tablets, teas, and extracts.

4.1.1 Roles in Natural Healing

Herbs play several roles in natural healing:

Immune system support: Many herbs, such as echinacea, astragalus, and garlic, are used for immune system support, helping to protect the body from infections and diseases.

Anti-inflammatory effects: Some herbs, such as turmeric, ginger, and boswellia, have anti-inflammatory effects, reducing inflammation and pain.
Stress relief: Herbs such as ashwagandha, valerian, and passionflower are used for stress relief and to promote relaxation.
Digestive health: Herbs such as peppermint, ginger, and fennel are used for digestive health, helping to relieve bloating, gas, and indigestion.

4.1.2 Benefits of Taking Herbal Supplements

Taking herbal supplements can have several benefits for natural healing:

Enhanced immune system function: Herbal supplements can help support immune system function, reducing the risk of infections and diseases.
Reduced inflammation and pain: Herbal supplements with anti-inflammatory effects can help reduce inflammation and pain, improving overall health and well-being.
Stress relief and relaxation: Herbal supplements for stress relief can help promote relaxation and improve mental health.
Improved digestive health: Herbal supplements for digestive health can help relieve digestive symptoms, such as bloating and gas.

4.2 Amino Acids

Amino acids are the building blocks of proteins and play many important roles in the body, including muscle growth and repair, brain function, and hormone production. Some common amino acids used for natural healing include:

L-lysine: Used for immune system support and to reduce the symptoms of cold sores.
L-arginine: Used for cardiovascular health and to improve blood flow.
L-theanine: Used for stress relief and to promote relaxation.
Glutamine: Used for muscle growth and repair, digestive health, and immune system support.

Amino acid supplements are available in various forms, including capsules, tablets, and powders.

4.2.1 Roles in Natural Healing

Amino acids play several roles in natural healing:

Muscle growth and repair: Amino acids, such as glutamine, are important for muscle growth and repair, supporting athletic performance and recovery.
Immune system support: Amino acids, such as L-lysine, are used for immune system support, helping to protect the body from infections and diseases.
Brain function: Amino acids, such as L-theanine, can help promote relaxation and improve mental health.

4.2.2 Benefits of Taking Amino Acid Supplements

Taking amino acid supplements can have several benefits for natural healing:

Enhanced athletic performance and recovery: Amino acid supplements can help support muscle growth and repair, improving athletic performance and recovery.
Improved immune system function: Amino acid supplements can help support immune system function, reducing the risk of infections and diseases.
Stress relief and relaxation: Amino acid supplements, such as L-theanine, can help promote relaxation and improve mental health.

4.3 Probiotics

Probiotics are live microorganisms that are beneficial for digestive health and immune system function. They are found in many fermented foods, such as yogurt, kefir, and sauerkraut, and are also available in various forms as supplements, including capsules and powders.

4.3.1 Roles in Natural Healing

Probiotics play several roles in natural healing:

Digestive health: Probiotics help maintain a healthy balance of bacteria in the gut, reducing the risk of digestive symptoms, such as bloating and gas.

Immune system function: Probiotics support immune system function, helping to protect the body from infections and diseases.

4.3.2 Benefits of Taking Probiotic Supplements

Taking probiotic supplements can have several benefits for natural healing:

Improved digestive health: Probiotic supplements can help maintain a healthy balance of bacteria in the gut, reducing the risk of digestive symptoms, such as bloating and gas.

Enhanced immune system function: Probiotic supplements can help support immune system function, reducing the risk of infections and diseases.

Protection against certain health conditions: Probiotic supplements may help protect against certain health conditions, such as irritable bowel syndrome (IBS), inflammatory bowel disease (IBD), and allergies.

4.4 Combination Supplements

Combination supplements are supplements that contain a combination of vitamins, minerals, herbs, amino acids, and/or probiotics. These supplements are often designed to target specific health concerns, such as immune system support, stress relief, or joint health. Examples of combination supplements include:

Multivitamins: Supplements that contain a combination of vitamins and minerals, designed to provide a daily dose of essential nutrients.

Joint health supplements: Supplements that contain a combination of vitamins, minerals, and herbs, designed to support joint health and reduce inflammation.

Immune system support supplements: Supplements that contain a combination of vitamins, minerals, and herbs, designed to support immune system function and reduce the risk of infections and diseases.

4.4.1 Roles in Natural Healing

Combination supplements play several roles in natural healing:

Targeted health support: Combination supplements are designed to target specific health concerns, providing a combination of nutrients and herbs that work together to support overall health and well-being.

Convenience: Combination supplements can be a convenient way to get a variety of nutrients in one easy-to-take supplement.

4.4.2 Benefits of Taking Combination Supplements

Taking combination supplements can have several benefits for natural healing:

Targeted health support: Combination supplements can provide targeted support for specific health concerns, such as joint health, immune system support, or stress relief.

Convenience: Combination supplements can be a convenient way to get a variety of nutrients in one easy-to-take supplement.

Cost-effective: Combination supplements can be a cost-effective way to get multiple nutrients, as opposed to purchasing several individual supplements.

Conclusion:

Vitamins, minerals, and supplements can play important roles in natural healing, providing essential nutrients that support immune system function, promote healthy aging, and reduce the risk of chronic diseases. By understanding the roles and benefits of different vitamins, minerals, herbs, amino acids, and probiotics, individuals can make informed decisions about which supplements to take to support their overall health and well-being. It is important to remember that supplements should not replace a healthy diet and lifestyle, and individuals should always consult with a healthcare professional before starting any new supplement regimen.

Treating Digestive Issues

Natural remedies for heartburn, indigestion, and acid reflux

Heartburn, indigestion, and acid reflux are some of the most common gastrointestinal problems that many people face on a daily basis. These conditions can be caused by several factors, including poor diet, stress, and certain medications. While many over-the-counter and prescription medications are available to treat these conditions, natural remedies can also be very effective. In this chapter, we will explore some of the best natural remedies for heartburn, indigestion, and acid reflux.

Understanding Heartburn, Indigestion, and Acid Reflux:

Before we discuss natural remedies, it is essential to understand these conditions. Heartburn is a burning sensation in the chest or throat, caused by stomach acid backing up into the esophagus. Indigestion is a general term used to describe discomfort in the upper abdomen after eating. Acid reflux occurs when stomach acid flows back into the esophagus, causing heartburn and other symptoms.

Causes of Heartburn, Indigestion, and Acid Reflux:

Several factors can contribute to these conditions. Some of the common causes include:

Eating large meals
Consuming acidic or spicy foods
Drinking alcohol or caffeine
Smoking
Stress
Certain medications such as aspirin or ibuprofen
Natural Remedies for Heartburn, Indigestion, and Acid Reflux:

Ginger:
Ginger is a well-known natural remedy for gastrointestinal problems, including heartburn, indigestion, and acid reflux. Ginger contains compounds called gingerols and shogaols, which have anti-inflammatory properties and

can help reduce inflammation in the stomach and esophagus.

How to use: You can use fresh ginger or ginger supplements. You can add grated ginger to your tea or food, or take ginger supplements in the form of capsules or tablets.

Apple Cider Vinegar:

Apple cider vinegar (ACV) is another natural remedy that can help reduce heartburn and acid reflux. ACV contains acetic acid, which can help balance the pH level in the stomach and reduce acid reflux.

How to use: Mix 1-2 tablespoons of ACV with water or juice and drink it before meals. You can also add honey to the mixture for taste.

Aloe Vera Juice:

Aloe vera juice is a popular natural remedy for heartburn and acid reflux. Aloe vera contains compounds called polysaccharides, which can help reduce inflammation and soothe the lining of the stomach and esophagus.

How to use: Drink ¼ to ½ cup of aloe vera juice before meals. You can also add it to smoothies or juices.

Slippery Elm:

Slippery elm is a herb that has been used for centuries to treat gastrointestinal problems, including heartburn and acid reflux. Slippery elm contains mucilage, a substance that can help soothe the lining of the esophagus and stomach.

How to use: Mix 1-2 teaspoons of slippery elm powder with water and drink it before meals.

Chamomile Tea:

Chamomile tea is another natural remedy that can help reduce heartburn and acid reflux. Chamomile contains compounds that can help reduce inflammation and relax the muscles in the digestive tract.

How to use: Drink chamomile tea before or after meals.

Baking Soda:

Baking soda is a natural antacid that can help neutralize stomach acid and reduce heartburn and acid reflux symptoms.

How to use: Mix ½ to 1 teaspoon of baking soda with water and drink it. Do not use this remedy if you are on a low-sodium diet or have high blood pressure.

Licorice:
Licorice is a herb that can help soothe the lining of the stomach and esophagus and reduce inflammation.

How to use: Drink licorice tea or take licorice supplements. However, licorice supplements can have side effects and should be taken only under the supervision of a healthcare professional.

Probiotics:
Probiotics are beneficial bacteria that can help improve digestion and reduce inflammation in the gut. Studies have shown that taking probiotics can help reduce symptoms of acid reflux and improve overall gut health.

How to use: Take probiotic supplements or consume probiotic-rich foods such as yogurt, kefir, sauerkraut, and kimchi.

DGL Licorice:
DGL licorice is a special form of licorice that has been processed to remove the compound glycyrrhizin, which can cause side effects. DGL licorice can help soothe the lining of the stomach and esophagus and reduce inflammation.

How to use: Take DGL licorice supplements before meals. However, like all supplements, DGL licorice should be taken under the supervision of a healthcare professional.

Lifestyle Changes:
In addition to natural remedies, making lifestyle changes can also help reduce symptoms of heartburn, indigestion, and acid reflux. Some of the lifestyle changes you can make include:

Eating smaller, more frequent meals
Avoiding spicy, fatty, and acidic foods
Avoiding alcohol and caffeine
Quitting smoking

Managing stress through techniques such as yoga, meditation, and deep breathing
Elevating the head of your bed to prevent stomach acid from flowing back into the esophagus
Conclusion:

Heartburn, indigestion, and acid reflux can be uncomfortable and disrupt your daily life. While there are many over-the-counter and prescription medications available to treat these conditions, natural remedies can also be effective. Ginger, apple cider vinegar, aloe vera juice, slippery elm, chamomile tea, baking soda, licorice, probiotics, DGL licorice, and lifestyle changes are all natural remedies that can help reduce symptoms of heartburn, indigestion, and acid reflux. However, if you have severe or persistent symptoms, it is essential to consult a healthcare professional to rule out any underlying medical conditions.

Herbal remedies for constipation and diarrhea

Herbal remedies have been used for centuries to treat a variety of ailments, including constipation and diarrhea. These natural remedies can provide relief without the harmful side effects of prescription medications. In this chapter, we will explore some of the most effective herbal remedies for constipation and diarrhea.

Constipation:

Constipation is a condition that affects millions of people worldwide. It is characterized by infrequent bowel movements, difficulty passing stools, and a feeling of incomplete evacuation. There are many factors that can contribute to constipation, including a low-fiber diet, dehydration, stress, and certain medications.

Psyllium Husk:
Psyllium husk is a popular herbal remedy for constipation. It is a form of soluble fiber that absorbs water and swells in the intestines,

helping to bulk up stools and promote bowel movements. Psyllium husk is available in various forms, including powder, capsules, and tablets.

To use psyllium husk for constipation, mix one teaspoon of the powder in a glass of water or juice and drink immediately. It is important to drink plenty of water when using psyllium husk, as it can cause dehydration if not consumed with enough water.

Senna:
Senna is a powerful herbal laxative that is commonly used to treat constipation. It contains compounds called anthraquinones, which stimulate the muscles of the intestines, helping to promote bowel movements.

Senna is available in various forms, including tea, capsules, and tablets. To use senna for constipation, brew a cup of senna tea or take one to two tablets or capsules before bed. It is important to follow the recommended dosage and not use senna for more than seven days in a row, as it can cause dependence and damage the intestinal lining.

Flaxseed:
Flaxseed is another effective herbal remedy for constipation. It contains both soluble and insoluble fiber, which helps to promote bowel movements and prevent constipation. Flaxseed also contains lignans, which have anti-inflammatory properties that can help to reduce inflammation in the intestines.

To use flaxseed for constipation, mix one tablespoon of ground flaxseed in a glass of water or sprinkle it on your cereal or yogurt. It is important to drink plenty of water when using flaxseed, as it can cause dehydration if not consumed with enough water.

Diarrhea:

Diarrhea is a condition that is characterized by loose, watery stools that occur more frequently than usual. It can be caused by a variety of factors, including viral or bacterial infections, food intolerances, and medications. Herbal remedies can be effective in treating diarrhea by reducing inflammation in the intestines and promoting the growth of beneficial gut bacteria.

Ginger:

Ginger is a popular herbal remedy for diarrhea. It contains compounds called gingerols and shogaols, which have anti-inflammatory properties that can help to reduce inflammation in the intestines. Ginger can also help to stimulate the production of digestive enzymes, which can help to break down food more efficiently.

To use ginger for diarrhea, brew a cup of ginger tea or take ginger capsules or tablets. It is important to follow the recommended dosage and not exceed four grams of ginger per day, as it can cause heartburn and stomach upset.

Peppermint:

Peppermint is another effective herbal remedy for diarrhea. It contains menthol, which has antispasmodic properties that can help to reduce cramping in the intestines. Peppermint can also help to stimulate the production of digestive enzymes and promote the growth of beneficial gut bacteria.

To use peppermint for diarrhea, brew a cup of peppermint tea or take peppermint oil capsules or tablets. It is important to follow the recommended dosage and not exceed 0.2-0.4 mL of peppermint oil per day, as it can cause heartburn and allergic reactions in some people.

Chamomile:

Chamomile is a gentle herbal remedy that can be used to treat diarrhea. It contains compounds called flavonoids, which have anti-inflammatory properties that can help to reduce inflammation in the intestines. Chamomile can also help to soothe the digestive system and promote the growth of beneficial gut bacteria.

To use chamomile for diarrhea, brew a cup of chamomile tea or take chamomile capsules or tablets. It is important to follow the recommended dosage and not exceed four grams of chamomile per day, as it can cause allergic reactions in some people.

Conclusion:

Herbal remedies can be effective in treating both constipation and diarrhea. Psyllium husk, senna, and flaxseed are effective herbal remedies for constipation, while ginger, peppermint, and chamomile are effective herbal remedies for diarrhea. It is important to follow the recommended dosage and consult a healthcare professional before using any herbal remedies, especially if you are pregnant, breastfeeding, or taking medications. With the right herbal remedies, you can find relief from constipation and diarrhea without the harmful side effects of prescription medications.

How to soothe an upset stomach naturally

An upset stomach can be a frustrating and uncomfortable experience. Whether you are experiencing indigestion, bloating, nausea, or other digestive issues, there are natural remedies that can help soothe your symptoms. In this chapter, we will explore several natural remedies to help ease an upset stomach.

Ginger

Ginger is a powerful natural remedy for upset stomachs. It contains compounds called gingerols and shogaols that help reduce inflammation and ease digestion. Ginger can also help relieve nausea and vomiting.

One way to use ginger is to make ginger tea. Simply slice a few pieces of fresh ginger root and add them to a pot of boiling water. Allow the tea to steep for a few minutes, then strain and drink. You can also add honey or lemon juice to the tea to improve the taste.

Another way to use ginger is to chew on a small piece of fresh ginger root. This can help relieve nausea and indigestion.

Peppermint

Peppermint is another natural remedy that can help soothe an upset stomach. It contains menthol, which helps relax the muscles in the digestive tract and ease digestion. Peppermint can also help relieve nausea and bloating.

One way to use peppermint is to drink peppermint tea. You can make peppermint tea by steeping fresh or dried peppermint leaves in boiling water for a few minutes, then straining and drinking. You can also add honey or lemon juice to the tea to improve the taste.

Another way to use peppermint is to chew on peppermint leaves or take a peppermint oil supplement. This can help relieve bloating and indigestion.

Chamomile

Chamomile is a gentle natural remedy that can help soothe an upset stomach. It contains compounds called flavonoids that help reduce inflammation and ease digestion. Chamomile can also help relieve nausea and cramping.

One way to use chamomile is to make chamomile tea. You can make chamomile tea by steeping fresh or dried chamomile flowers in boiling water for a few minutes, then straining and drinking. You can also add honey or lemon juice to the tea to improve the taste.

Another way to use chamomile is to take a chamomile supplement. This can help relieve cramping and indigestion.

Fennel

Fennel is a natural remedy that can help relieve gas and bloating. It contains compounds called anethole and fenchone that help relax the muscles in the digestive tract and ease digestion. Fennel can also help relieve nausea and cramping.

One way to use fennel is to make fennel tea. You can make fennel tea by steeping fresh or dried fennel seeds in boiling water for a few minutes, then straining and drinking. You can also add honey or lemon juice to the tea to improve the taste.

Another way to use fennel is to chew on fennel seeds after a meal. This can help relieve gas and bloating.

Apple Cider Vinegar

Apple cider vinegar is a natural remedy that can help balance the pH levels in the stomach and improve digestion. It contains acetic acid, which helps stimulate the production of digestive enzymes. Apple cider vinegar can also help relieve heartburn and acid reflux.

One way to use apple cider vinegar is to mix one tablespoon of apple cider vinegar with a glass of water and drink it before a meal. You can also add honey to the mixture to improve the taste.

Another way to use apple cider vinegar is to take an apple cider vinegar supplement. This can help relieve heartburn and acid reflux.

Bananas

Bananas are a natural remedy that can help soothe an upset stomach. They are high in potassium, which helps regulate the fluid balance in the body and can help relieve bloating. Bananas are also easy to digest and can help relieve nausea.

One way to use bananas is to eat a ripe banana. This can help relieve nausea and improve digestion.

Another way to use bananas is to make a banana smoothie. Simply blend a ripe banana with some almond milk or yogurt, and add a spoonful of honey or cinnamon for extra flavor. This can help soothe an upset stomach and provide some relief from digestive issues.

Probiotics

Probiotics are live bacteria and yeasts that can help improve the health of the digestive system. They can help regulate the balance of bacteria in the gut and improve digestion. Probiotics can also help relieve bloating, gas, and other digestive issues.

One way to use probiotics is to eat foods that are rich in probiotics, such as yogurt, kefir, sauerkraut, kimchi, or kombucha. These foods contain live bacteria that can help improve digestive health.

Another way to use probiotics is to take a probiotic supplement. These supplements contain a concentrated dose of probiotics that can help improve digestive health.

Hydration

Staying hydrated is an important part of maintaining digestive health. Drinking plenty of water can help regulate the fluid balance in the body and improve digestion. It can also help relieve constipation and bloating.

One way to stay hydrated is to drink water throughout the day. Aim to drink at least 8 glasses of water per day, and more if you are exercising or sweating.

Another way to stay hydrated is to eat foods that are high in water content, such as watermelon, cucumbers, or celery. These foods can help provide hydration and improve digestive health.

Rest and relaxation

Rest and relaxation are important for maintaining digestive health. Stress and anxiety can have a negative impact on digestive health and can cause digestive issues such as bloating, indigestion, and constipation. Taking time to relax and rest can help improve digestive health and reduce digestive issues.

One way to rest and relax is to practice deep breathing exercises or meditation. These practices can help reduce stress and promote relaxation.

Another way to rest and relax is to take a warm bath or use a heating pad on the stomach. This can help relax the muscles in the digestive tract and promote digestion.

In conclusion, an upset stomach can be a frustrating and uncomfortable experience. However, there are several natural remedies that can help soothe digestive issues such as bloating, nausea, and indigestion. Ginger, peppermint, chamomile, fennel, apple cider vinegar, bananas, probiotics, hydration, and rest and relaxation are all natural remedies that can help improve digestive health and provide relief from digestive issues. Incorporating these remedies into your daily routine can help soothe an upset stomach naturally and improve overall digestive health.

Relieving Pain and Inflammation

Natural remedies for joint pain and arthritis

Joint pain and arthritis affect millions of people worldwide, and the conventional treatments for these conditions are often expensive and come with unwanted side effects. Fortunately, there are natural remedies that can help relieve joint pain and arthritis symptoms without the negative consequences of pharmaceutical drugs. In this chapter, we will discuss some of the most effective natural remedies for joint pain and arthritis.

Dietary Changes

One of the most effective natural remedies for joint pain and arthritis is dietary changes. Certain foods can trigger inflammation in the body, exacerbating joint pain and arthritis symptoms. Therefore, avoiding these foods and consuming anti-inflammatory foods can significantly reduce joint pain.

Foods to avoid include processed foods, refined sugar, and saturated and trans fats. These foods can cause inflammation and worsen joint pain. On the other hand, foods that are high in omega-3 fatty acids, such as fatty fish, nuts, and seeds, can help reduce inflammation and ease joint pain. Other anti-inflammatory foods include fruits and vegetables, whole grains, and spices such as turmeric and ginger.

Supplements

Several supplements have been shown to be effective in relieving joint pain and arthritis symptoms. Glucosamine and chondroitin supplements are popular options, as they are believed to help rebuild cartilage in the joints. Other supplements that may help reduce joint pain include omega-3 fatty acids, vitamin D, and curcumin, which is found in turmeric.

Before taking any supplements, it is important to speak with a healthcare provider to ensure they are safe and effective for you.

Exercise

While exercise may seem counterintuitive for those experiencing joint pain, it can actually be incredibly beneficial. Exercise helps strengthen the muscles around the joints, reducing the pressure on the joints and alleviating pain. Low-impact exercises such as swimming, cycling, and yoga are great options for those with joint pain.

Additionally, regular exercise helps maintain a healthy weight, which is important for joint health. Excess weight puts added pressure on the joints, which can worsen joint pain and increase the risk of developing arthritis.

Massage Therapy

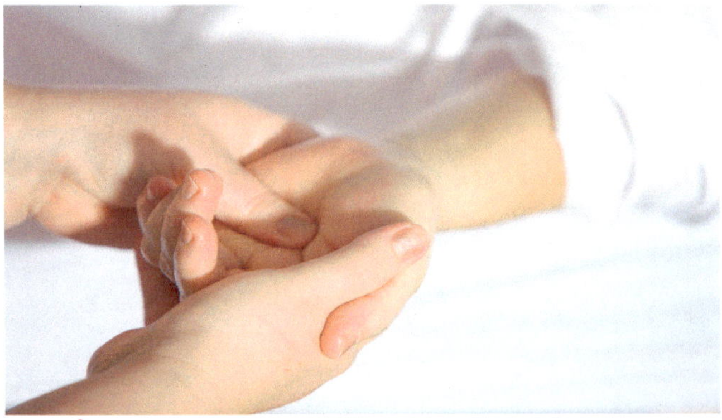

Massage therapy is another natural remedy that can help relieve joint pain and arthritis symptoms. Massage helps increase blood flow and reduce inflammation in the joints. Additionally, massage can help reduce stress, which can worsen joint pain.

Acupuncture

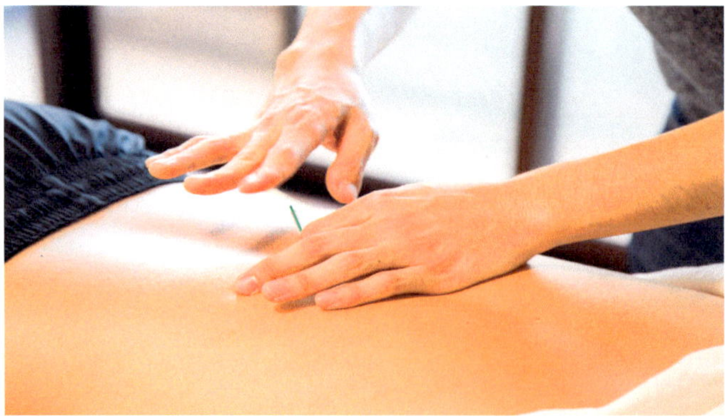

Acupuncture is an ancient Chinese healing practice that involves inserting thin needles into specific points on the body. It has been shown to be effective in reducing joint pain and inflammation in those with arthritis. While the exact mechanisms behind acupuncture are not fully understood, it is believed to stimulate the body's natural healing processes.

Heat and Cold Therapy

Heat and cold therapy are simple and effective natural remedies for joint pain and arthritis. Heat therapy helps increase blood flow to the joints, which can reduce pain and stiffness. Heat can be applied in several ways, such as with a hot water bottle, heating pad, or warm bath.

Cold therapy, on the other hand, helps reduce inflammation and numb pain. Cold can be applied using a cold pack, ice wrapped in a towel, or a bag of frozen vegetables.

Conclusion

Joint pain and arthritis can be debilitating conditions that greatly impact a person's quality of life. However, there are natural remedies that can help relieve symptoms without the negative side effects of pharmaceutical drugs. By making dietary changes, taking supplements, engaging in regular exercise, receiving massage therapy or acupuncture, and using heat and cold therapy, those with joint pain and arthritis can experience relief and improved joint health. As always, it is important to speak with a healthcare provider before starting any new treatment regimen.

Herbal remedies for headaches and migraines

Headaches and migraines are common ailments that can cause a significant amount of discomfort, pain, and disruption in a person's life. While there are many over-the-counter medications available to treat these conditions, some people prefer to use natural remedies. In this chapter, we will explore some of the most effective herbal remedies for headaches and migraines.

Herbal Remedies for Headaches and Migraines

Feverfew

Feverfew is a medicinal herb that has been used for centuries to treat various ailments, including headaches and migraines. The active ingredient in feverfew, parthenolide, has been shown to reduce inflammation and prevent the constriction of blood vessels in the brain. This herb is available in various forms, including capsules, tablets, and tinctures.

Butterbur

Butterbur is another herbal remedy that has been used for centuries to treat headaches and migraines. The active ingredient in butterbur, petasin, has been shown to reduce inflammation and prevent the constriction of blood vessels in the brain. Butterbur is available in various forms, including capsules, tablets, and tinctures.

Peppermint

Peppermint is a refreshing herb that has been used for centuries to treat headaches and migraines. The menthol in peppermint has a cooling effect that can help to reduce pain and inflammation. Peppermint can be used in various forms, including tea, essential oil, and capsules.

Ginger

Ginger is a root that has been used for centuries to treat various ailments, including headaches and migraines. The active compounds in ginger, gingerols and shogaols, have anti-inflammatory and analgesic properties that can help to reduce pain and inflammation. Ginger can be used in various forms, including tea, capsules, and essential oil.

Willow Bark

Willow bark is a natural pain reliever that has been used for centuries to treat headaches and migraines. The active ingredient in willow bark, salicin, is similar to aspirin and can help to reduce pain and inflammation. Willow bark is available in various forms, including capsules, tablets, and tinctures.

Lavender

Lavender is a calming herb that has been used for centuries to treat headaches and migraines. The essential oil of lavender has a relaxing effect that can help to reduce pain and inflammation. Lavender can be used in various forms, including essential oil, capsules, and tea.

Chamomile

Chamomile is a soothing herb that has been used for centuries to treat various ailments, including headaches and migraines. The active compounds in chamomile, chamazulene, and apigenin, have anti-inflammatory and analgesic properties that can help to reduce pain and inflammation. Chamomile can be used in various forms, including tea, capsules, and essential oil.

Valerian Root

Valerian root is a calming herb that has been used for centuries to treat headaches and migraines. The active compounds in valerian root, valerenic acid, and valeranone, have a relaxing effect that can help to reduce pain and inflammation. Valerian root is available in various forms, including capsules, tablets, and tinctures.

Passionflower

Passionflower is a calming herb that has been used for centuries to treat various ailments, including headaches and migraines. The active compounds in passionflower, flavonoids, and alkaloids, have a relaxing effect that can help to reduce pain and inflammation. Passionflower can be used in various forms, including tea, capsules, and tinctures.

Ginkgo Biloba

Ginkgo biloba is a medicinal herb that has been used for centuries to improve cognitive function and circulation. It can also be used as an herbal remedy for headaches and migraines. The active compounds in ginkgo biloba, terpenoids, and flavonoids, have anti-inflammatory and antioxidant properties that can help to reduce pain and inflammation. Ginkgo biloba is available in various forms, including capsules and tablets.

Eucalyptus

Eucalyptus is a refreshing herb that has been used for centuries to treat headaches and migraines. The essential oil of eucalyptus has a cooling effect that can help to reduce pain and inflammation. Eucalyptus can be used in various forms, including essential oil, capsules, and tea.

Rosemary

Rosemary is an herb that has been used for centuries to treat headaches and migraines. The essential oil of rosemary has a stimulating effect that can help to improve circulation and reduce pain and inflammation. Rosemary can be used in various forms, including essential oil, capsules, and tea.

White Willow

White willow is a natural pain reliever that has been used for centuries to treat headaches and migraines. The active ingredient in white willow, salicin, is similar to aspirin and can help to reduce pain and inflammation. White willow is available in various forms, including capsules, tablets, and tinctures.

St. John's Wort

St. John's wort is an herb that has been used for centuries to treat various ailments, including headaches and migraines. The active compounds in St. John's wort, hypericin, and hyperforin, have anti-inflammatory and antidepressant properties that can help to reduce pain and inflammation. St. John's wort can be used in various forms, including capsules, tablets, and tinctures.

Catnip

Catnip is an herb that has been used for centuries to treat headaches and migraines. The active compounds in catnip, nepetalactone, and nepetalic acid, have a calming effect that can help to reduce pain and inflammation. Catnip can be used in various forms, including tea and essential oil.

Conclusion

Headaches and migraines can be debilitating and can significantly impact a person's quality of life. While there are many over-the-counter medications available to treat these conditions, some people prefer to use natural remedies. Herbal remedies such as feverfew, butterbur, peppermint, ginger, willow bark, lavender, chamomile, valerian root, passionflower, ginkgo biloba, eucalyptus, rosemary, white willow, St. John's wort, and catnip have been shown to be effective in treating headaches and migraines. It is important to consult with a healthcare provider before using any herbal remedies, especially if you are pregnant, breastfeeding, or taking any medications.

Homeopathic remedies for menstrual cramps

Menstrual cramps, also known as dysmenorrhea, are a common ailment experienced by women during their menstrual cycle. While over-the-counter pain relievers are commonly used to alleviate the pain, many women are seeking natural remedies to manage their menstrual cramps. Homeopathic remedies have been shown to be an effective and safe alternative to traditional pain medication. In this chapter, we will discuss the top homeopathic remedies for menstrual cramps and their benefits.

What is Homeopathy?

Homeopathy is a form of alternative medicine that originated in Germany in the late 18th century. It is based on the principle of "like cures like," which means that a substance that causes symptoms in a healthy person can be used to treat similar symptoms in a sick person. Homeopathic remedies are made from natural substances such as plants, minerals, and animals. The substances are diluted and succussed (shaken vigorously) to create a potentized remedy.

How Homeopathic Remedies Work for Menstrual Cramps

Homeopathic remedies work by stimulating the body's natural healing mechanisms. They are believed to help restore balance and harmony to the body, which can help alleviate symptoms of menstrual cramps. Homeopathic remedies are selected based on the individual's specific symptoms, which means that each remedy is tailored to the individual's unique needs. The remedies are safe, non-toxic, and do not have any side effects.

Top Homeopathic Remedies for Menstrual Cramps:

Magnesia phosphorica: This remedy is often used for menstrual cramps that are relieved by heat. The cramps may be accompanied by shooting, stabbing pains that feel better with warmth. The person may also experience a headache or feel weak and tired.

Sepia: This remedy is often used for menstrual cramps that are accompanied by a heavy feeling in the pelvis. The person may feel irritable, sad, or indifferent. They may also experience back pain and fatigue.

Pulsatilla: This remedy is often used for menstrual cramps that are accompanied by a changeable mood. The person may feel weepy, emotional, or clingy. They may also experience a headache, nausea, or diarrhea.

Belladonna: This remedy is often used for menstrual cramps that are accompanied by intense, throbbing pain. The pain may come and go suddenly and may be worse on the right side of the body. The person may also have a fever, red face, and dilated pupils.

Chamomilla: This remedy is often used for menstrual cramps that are accompanied by irritability and anger. The person may be extremely sensitive to pain and may feel better with warmth. They may also experience diarrhea or vomiting.

Caulophyllum: This remedy is often used for menstrual cramps that are accompanied by irregular or painful periods. The person may also experience joint pain and stiffness.

Cimicifuga: This remedy is often used for menstrual cramps that are accompanied by a sharp, shooting pain in the pelvis. The person may also experience mood swings, anxiety, and depression.

Lachesis: This remedy is often used for menstrual cramps that are worse on the left side of the body. The person may also experience hot flashes, palpitations, and irritability.

How to Use Homeopathic Remedies for Menstrual Cramps:

Homeopathic remedies are available in various forms, including pellets, tablets, and liquids. They should be taken as directed on the label or as prescribed by a qualified homeopath. It is important to avoid touching the remedies with your hands as this can reduce their effectiveness. Instead, use the cap of the container or a clean spoon to dispense the remedy.

It is recommended to take the remedy as soon as symptoms begin to appear, and to repeat the dose as necessary. In general, homeopathic remedies should be taken at least 15 minutes before or after eating or drinking, as well as avoiding strong flavors such as mint or coffee, which can interfere with their absorption.

In addition to using homeopathic remedies, there are other natural remedies that can help alleviate menstrual cramps, such as:

Heat therapy: Applying heat to the lower abdomen can help relax the muscles and reduce pain. A hot water bottle or heating pad can be used for this purpose.

Exercise: Regular exercise, such as yoga or walking, can help improve circulation and reduce muscle tension.

Diet: A diet rich in fruits, vegetables, whole grains, and lean protein can help reduce inflammation and improve overall health.

Herbal remedies: Certain herbs, such as ginger, turmeric, and cinnamon, have anti-inflammatory properties that can help alleviate menstrual cramps.

Stress reduction: Stress can exacerbate menstrual cramps, so finding ways to reduce stress, such as through meditation or deep breathing, can be helpful.

Conclusion:

Homeopathic remedies offer a safe and effective alternative to traditional pain medication for menstrual cramps. By addressing the individual's specific symptoms, homeopathic remedies can help restore balance and harmony to the body and alleviate menstrual cramps. However, it is important to work with a qualified homeopath to ensure proper selection and dosing of remedies. In addition to homeopathic remedies, other natural remedies, such as heat therapy, exercise, and herbal remedies, can also help alleviate menstrual cramps.

Boosting Immunity and Preventing Illness

Vitamins and supplements for immune support

The immune system is a complex network of cells, tissues, and organs that work together to defend the body against harmful invaders such as bacteria, viruses, and other pathogens. A strong immune system is essential for good health, as it can help prevent illness and fight off infections. Vitamins and supplements can play a significant role in supporting the immune system and keeping it functioning optimally. In this chapter, we will explore the various vitamins and supplements that can help boost immunity and provide effective remedies for common ailments.

Vitamin C

Vitamin C is an essential nutrient that plays a vital role in immune function. It is a potent antioxidant that can protect cells from damage caused by free radicals, which are unstable molecules that can contribute to disease and aging. Vitamin C can also help to stimulate the production of white blood cells, which are crucial for fighting infections.

Research has shown that taking vitamin C supplements can reduce the duration and severity of colds and flu. It can also help to enhance the function of the skin's barrier, which can help prevent infections from entering the body. Good sources of vitamin C include citrus fruits, berries, kiwi, peppers, and leafy greens.

Vitamin D

Vitamin D is another essential nutrient that plays a critical role in immune function. It helps to regulate the immune system by controlling the expression of genes involved in immune function. Research has shown that low levels of vitamin D are associated with an increased risk of respiratory infections, such as colds and flu.

Supplementing with vitamin D may help to reduce the risk of respiratory infections, particularly in people who are deficient in this nutrient. Good sources of vitamin D include fatty fish, eggs, and fortified dairy products.

However, it can be challenging to get enough vitamin D from food alone, especially during the winter months when sunlight exposure is limited. Therefore, supplementation may be necessary.

Zinc

Zinc is an essential mineral that plays a vital role in immune function. It is necessary for the development and function of immune cells and can help to stimulate the production of antibodies. Research has shown that zinc can help to reduce the duration and severity of colds and flu.

Good sources of zinc include meat, shellfish, legumes, nuts, and seeds. However, it can be challenging to get enough zinc from food alone, especially for vegetarians and vegans. Therefore, supplementation may be necessary.

Echinacea

Echinacea is a popular herbal supplement that has been used for centuries to support immune function. It is believed to work by stimulating the production of white blood cells, which are crucial for fighting infections. Research has shown that echinacea can help to reduce the duration and severity of colds and flu.

Echinacea is available in various forms, including teas, capsules, and extracts. However, it is essential to choose a high-quality product that contains the active ingredients found in the plant.

Probiotics

Probiotics are live bacteria and yeasts that are beneficial for health. They can help to support immune function by promoting the growth of beneficial bacteria in the gut, which can help to prevent infections from harmful bacteria and viruses. Probiotics have been shown to be particularly effective in reducing the risk of respiratory infections in children.

Probiotics are found naturally in fermented foods such as yogurt, kefir, sauerkraut, and kimchi. However, supplementation may be necessary, especially for people who do not consume these foods regularly.

Garlic

Garlic is a potent antimicrobial agent that has been used for centuries to treat infections. It contains compounds that can help to boost immune function and fight off infections. Research has shown that garlic can help to reduce the duration and severity of colds and flu.

Garlic is available in various forms, including capsules, tablets, and extracts. It can also be used fresh in cooking to add flavor and health benefits to meals.

Vitamin E

Vitamin E is a potent antioxidant that can help to protect cells from damage caused by free radicals. It is also involved in immune function and can help to support the production of white blood cells. Research has shown that supplementing with vitamin E can help to improve immune function in older adults.

Good sources of vitamin E include nuts, seeds, vegetable oils, and leafy greens. However, it can be challenging to get enough vitamin E from food alone, especially for people who do not consume a varied diet. Therefore, supplementation may be necessary.

Astragalus

Astragalus is a herb that has been used in traditional Chinese medicine for centuries to support immune function. It is believed to work by stimulating the production of white blood cells and increasing the activity of natural killer cells, which are crucial for fighting infections. Research has shown that astragalus can help to reduce the duration and severity of colds and flu.

Astragalus is available in various forms, including teas, capsules, and extracts. However, it is essential to choose a high-quality product that contains the active ingredients found in the plant.

Selenium

Selenium is an essential mineral that plays a vital role in immune function. It can help to enhance the activity of white blood cells and increase the production of antibodies. Research has shown that selenium can help to reduce the risk of respiratory infections, particularly in people who are deficient in this nutrient.

Good sources of selenium include Brazil nuts, seafood, meat, and poultry. However, it can be challenging to get enough selenium from food alone, especially for people who do not consume these foods regularly. Therefore, supplementation may be necessary.

Conclusion

Vitamins and supplements can play a significant role in supporting immune function and providing effective remedies for common ailments. Vitamin C, vitamin D, zinc, echinacea, probiotics, garlic, vitamin E, astragalus, and selenium are all beneficial for immune support. However, it is essential to choose high-quality products and follow recommended dosages to avoid adverse effects. A healthy and balanced diet, regular exercise, and adequate sleep are also crucial for maintaining a strong immune system.

Herbal remedies for preventing and treating the common cold and flu

The common cold and flu are viral infections that affect millions of people every year. Symptoms of these illnesses include coughing, sneezing, congestion, sore throat, and fatigue. While there is no cure for the common cold or flu, there are many natural remedies that can help alleviate symptoms and prevent these illnesses from occurring. In this chapter, we will discuss herbal remedies that can be used to prevent and treat the common cold and flu.

Echinacea

Echinacea is a popular herb that is often used to prevent and treat the common cold and flu. This herb contains compounds that can help boost the immune system and fight off infections. Echinacea is available in many forms, including tea, tincture, and capsules. Drinking echinacea tea regularly or taking echinacea supplements can help prevent the common cold and flu, as well as alleviate symptoms.

Elderberry

Elderberry is another herbal remedy that is commonly used to treat the common cold and flu. This herb contains compounds that can help reduce inflammation and boost the immune system. Elderberry is available in many forms, including tea, tincture, and syrup. Drinking elderberry tea or taking elderberry syrup regularly can help prevent the common cold and flu, as well as alleviate symptoms.

Garlic

Garlic is a powerful herb that has been used for centuries to prevent and treat infections. This herb contains compounds that can help boost the immune system and fight off viruses and bacteria. Eating garlic regularly can help prevent the common cold and flu, as well as alleviate symptoms. Garlic supplements are also available for those who do not like the taste of garlic.

Ginger

Ginger is a popular herb that is often used to treat cold and flu symptoms. This herb contains compounds that can help reduce inflammation and boost the immune system. Drinking ginger tea or taking ginger supplements can help alleviate symptoms of the common cold and flu, such as coughing and congestion.

Licorice Root

Licorice root is an herb that is often used to soothe sore throats and reduce inflammation. This herb contains compounds that can help boost the immune system and fight off infections. Drinking licorice tea or taking licorice supplements can help alleviate symptoms of the common cold and flu, such as sore throat and coughing.

Peppermint

Peppermint is an herb that is often used to alleviate symptoms of the common cold and flu. This herb contains compounds that can help reduce inflammation and soothe sore throats. Drinking peppermint tea or inhaling peppermint oil can help alleviate symptoms of the common cold and flu, such as coughing and congestion.

Turmeric

Turmeric is an herb that is often used to reduce inflammation and boost the immune system. This herb contains compounds that can help fight off infections and reduce inflammation. Drinking turmeric tea or taking turmeric supplements can help prevent the common cold and flu, as well as alleviate symptoms.

Conclusion

Herbal remedies can be effective in preventing and treating the common cold and flu. Echinacea, elderberry, garlic, ginger, licorice root, peppermint, and turmeric are just a few of the many herbal remedies that can help alleviate symptoms and boost the immune system. Before using any herbal remedy, it is important to talk to your doctor to ensure that it is safe for you to use. If you are pregnant, nursing, or taking medication, you should also consult with your doctor before using any herbal remedies. With the right herbal remedies and proper care, you can prevent and treat the common cold and flu naturally.

Natural remedies for seasonal allergies

Seasonal allergies, also known as hay fever or allergic rhinitis, affect millions of people worldwide. Symptoms include sneezing, runny or stuffy nose, itchy or watery eyes, and itching in the nose or throat. These symptoms can be caused by an allergic reaction to pollen, dust mites, animal dander, or other environmental factors. While over-the-counter and prescription medications are commonly used to treat seasonal allergies, natural remedies can also be effective. This chapter will explore some of the natural remedies that can be used to alleviate seasonal allergy symptoms.

Natural Remedies for Seasonal Allergies

2.1. Saline Nasal Irrigation

Saline nasal irrigation involves rinsing the nasal passages with a saltwater solution. This can help to flush out irritants and allergens that are causing allergy symptoms. Saline nasal irrigation can be done using a neti pot, squeeze bottle, or nasal spray. To make a saltwater solution, mix 1/4 to 1/2 teaspoon of salt with 8 ounces of warm water. It is important to use distilled or boiled water to avoid the risk of infection.

2.2. Local Honey

Local honey is said to help alleviate seasonal allergy symptoms by exposing the body to small amounts of pollen. The theory is that over time, the body will become less reactive to pollen, reducing allergy symptoms. To use local honey as a natural remedy for seasonal allergies, take a teaspoon or two each day.

2.3. Quercetin

Quercetin is a plant flavonoid that has been shown to have anti-inflammatory properties. It is also an antioxidant and can help to stabilize mast cells, which are involved in the release of histamine during an allergic reaction. Quercetin can be found in foods such as apples, onions, and citrus fruits, but can also be taken as a supplement.

2.4. Butterbur

Butterbur is a plant that has been used for centuries as a natural remedy for seasonal allergies. It is thought to work by reducing inflammation and inhibiting the release of histamine. Butterbur can be taken as a supplement or in the form of an extract.

2.5. Stinging Nettle

Stinging nettle is a plant that has been used for centuries to treat allergies and other respiratory conditions. It contains histamine, which may seem counterintuitive, but can actually help to desensitize the body to pollen and other allergens. Stinging nettle can be taken as a supplement or brewed into a tea.

2.6. Vitamin C

Vitamin C is a powerful antioxidant that can help to reduce inflammation and boost the immune system. It may also help to reduce histamine levels in the body. Vitamin C can be found in foods such as oranges, strawberries, and broccoli, but can also be taken as a supplement.

2.7. Probiotics

Probiotics are beneficial bacteria that live in the gut. They have been shown to help regulate the immune system and reduce inflammation. This can be particularly helpful for people with seasonal allergies, as allergies are often caused by an overactive immune system. Probiotics can be found in foods such as yogurt, kefir, and sauerkraut, but can also be taken as a supplement.

2.8. Essential Oils

Essential oils such as peppermint, eucalyptus, and lavender can help to alleviate seasonal allergy symptoms. Peppermint oil can help to reduce inflammation and clear the sinuses. Eucalyptus oil can help to open up the airways and reduce congestion. Lavender oil can help to reduce inflammation and calm the nervous system. Essential oils can be diffused into the air, added to a warm bath, or diluted with a carrier oil and applied topically.

2.9. Acupuncture

Acupuncture is a traditional Chinese medicine technique that involves the insertion of thin needles into specific points on the body. It is thought to work by stimulating the body's natural healing processes and reducing inflammation. Some studies have shown that acupuncture can be an effective natural remedy for seasonal allergies.

2.10. Mind-Body Techniques

Stress can exacerbate seasonal allergy symptoms, so mind-body techniques such as meditation, deep breathing, and yoga can be helpful in reducing stress and promoting relaxation. These techniques can also help to reduce inflammation and boost the immune system.

Precautions and Considerations

While natural remedies can be effective in alleviating seasonal allergy symptoms, it is important to take precautions and consider potential risks. Some natural remedies, such as butterbur, may interact with certain medications or cause side effects. It is important to talk to a healthcare provider before starting any new natural remedies, especially if you are taking prescription medications or have a chronic health condition.

In addition, it is important to remember that natural remedies may not work for everyone. It may take some trial and error to find the right combination of remedies that work for your individual needs. It is also important to continue to practice good self-care habits, such as getting enough rest, staying hydrated, and avoiding allergens as much as possible.

Conclusion

Seasonal allergies can be a frustrating and uncomfortable condition, but natural remedies can offer an effective and safe alternative to traditional medications. Saline nasal irrigation, local honey, quercetin, butterbur, stinging nettle, vitamin C, probiotics, essential oils, acupuncture, and mind-body techniques are all natural remedies that can help to alleviate seasonal allergy symptoms. However, it is important to take precautions and consider potential risks, and to work with a healthcare provider to find the right combination of remedies for your individual needs.

Supporting Mental Health

Natural remedies for anxiety and depression

Anxiety and depression are among the most prevalent mental health disorders worldwide, affecting millions of people. These conditions are usually treated with medications, but natural remedies can also be effective in reducing symptoms. This chapter will explore the most effective natural remedies for anxiety and depression and provide a guide on how to use them.

Exercise

Exercise is one of the most effective natural remedies for anxiety and depression. Exercise can help reduce stress, boost mood, and increase self-esteem. Regular exercise has been shown to be as effective as medication in treating mild to moderate depression. Exercise also releases endorphins, the body's natural mood-boosting chemicals, which can help relieve anxiety and depression symptoms. Exercise can be as simple as a brisk walk or a bike ride, and it is recommended to do it for at least 30 minutes a day, five days a week.

Meditation

Meditation is an ancient practice that has been used for thousands of years to reduce stress and promote relaxation. Meditation involves sitting quietly and focusing on your breath, or a particular sound or mantra. Studies have shown that regular meditation can reduce symptoms of anxiety and depression, improve sleep quality, and lower blood pressure. There are many resources available for learning meditation, including books, apps, and online videos.

Yoga

Yoga is a form of exercise that combines physical postures with breathing techniques and meditation. Yoga has been shown to be an effective natural remedy for anxiety and depression. Yoga helps to reduce stress, improve mood, and increase flexibility and strength. Regular yoga practice can also improve sleep quality, reduce fatigue, and lower blood pressure.

Dietary changes

Dietary changes can also be effective in reducing symptoms of anxiety and depression. Eating a healthy, balanced diet can help improve mood and reduce stress. Foods that are rich in omega-3 fatty acids, such as salmon, tuna, and walnuts, have been shown to reduce symptoms of depression. Similarly, foods that are rich in vitamin B, such as leafy greens and whole grains, have been shown to improve mood and reduce stress.

Herbal remedies

Herbal remedies have been used for centuries to treat a variety of ailments, including anxiety and depression. The most effective herbs for treating these conditions include St. John's Wort, kava, and chamomile. St. John's Wort has been shown to be as effective as medication in treating mild to moderate depression. Kava is a natural sedative that can help reduce anxiety and promote relaxation. Chamomile is a natural relaxant that can help reduce anxiety and improve sleep quality.

Acupuncture

Acupuncture is an ancient Chinese practice that involves inserting thin needles into specific points on the body. Acupuncture has been shown to be an effective natural remedy for anxiety and depression. Acupuncture can help reduce stress, improve mood, and increase relaxation. Acupuncture is usually done by a licensed practitioner and can be done alone or in combination with other natural remedies.

Aromatherapy

Aromatherapy is a natural remedy that involves using essential oils to promote relaxation and reduce stress. Essential oils can be used in a diffuser, added to bathwater, or used in massage oil. The most effective essential oils for reducing anxiety and depression symptoms include lavender, bergamot, and chamomile. Lavender is known for its calming properties, while bergamot can help reduce anxiety and improve mood. Chamomile is a natural relaxant that can help improve sleep quality.

Conclusion

Natural remedies can be effective in reducing symptoms of anxiety and depression. Exercise, meditation, yoga, dietary changes, herbal remedies, acupuncture, and aromatherapy are all natural remedies that can help improve mood, reduce stress, and promote relaxation. It is essential to consult with a healthcare provider before starting any natural remedies for anxiety and depression

Herbal remedies for insomnia and sleep issues

Insomnia and sleep issues are common problems that affect millions of people worldwide. The lack of quality sleep can lead to fatigue, irritability, and difficulty concentrating. It can also increase the risk of developing health problems such as obesity, diabetes, and heart disease. While there are many prescription medications available for treating sleep problems, they can come with side effects and may not be appropriate for everyone. Herbal remedies offer a natural and safe alternative for promoting better sleep. In this chapter, we will explore some of the best herbal remedies for insomnia and sleep issues.

Valerian Root

Valerian root is a popular herbal remedy for sleep problems. It has been used for centuries as a natural sedative and has been shown to be effective in treating insomnia. Valerian root contains compounds that interact with the brain's GABA receptors, which help to calm the nervous system and promote relaxation. Studies have shown that valerian root can improve sleep quality and reduce the time it takes to fall asleep. Valerian root is available in many forms, including capsules, teas, and tinctures.

Chamomile

Chamomile is a popular herb that has been used for centuries for its calming and relaxing effects. It contains compounds that interact with the brain's GABA receptors, which help to promote relaxation and reduce anxiety. Chamomile has been shown to improve sleep quality and reduce the time it takes to fall asleep. It is available in many forms, including teas, capsules, and tinctures.

Passionflower

Passionflower is a plant that has been used for centuries for its calming effects. It contains compounds that interact with the brain's GABA receptors, which help to promote relaxation and reduce anxiety. Passionflower has been shown to improve sleep quality and reduce the time it takes to fall asleep. It is available in many forms, including teas, capsules, and tinctures.

Lavender

Lavender is a popular herb that has been used for centuries for its calming and relaxing effects. It contains compounds that interact with the brain's GABA receptors, which help to promote relaxation and reduce anxiety. Lavender has been shown to improve sleep quality and reduce the time it takes to fall asleep. It is available in many forms, including teas, essential oils, and tinctures.

Lemon Balm

Lemon balm is a plant that has been used for centuries for its calming and relaxing effects. It contains compounds that interact with the brain's GABA receptors, which help to promote relaxation and reduce anxiety. Lemon balm has been shown to improve sleep quality and reduce the time it takes to fall asleep. It is available in many forms, including teas, capsules, and tinctures.

Ashwagandha

Ashwagandha is an herb that has been used for centuries for its calming and rclaxing effects. It is an adaptogenic herb, which means it helps the body adapt to stress. Ashwagandha has been shown to improve sleep quality and reduce the time it takes to fall asleep. It is available in many forms, including teas, capsules, and tinctures.

Skullcap

Skullcap is a plant that has been used for centuries for its calming and relaxing effects. It contains compounds that interact with the brain's GABA receptors, which help to promote relaxation and reduce anxiety. Skullcap has been shown to improve sleep quality and reduce the time it takes to fall asleep. It is available in many forms, including teas, capsules, and tinctures.

Kava

Kava is a plant that has been used for centuries for its calming and relaxing effects. It contains compounds that interact with the brain's GABA receptors, which help to promote relaxation and reduce anxiety. Kava has been shown to improve sleep quality and reduce the time it takes to fall asleep. It is available in many forms, including teas, capsules, and tinctures. However, it's important to note that kava can have side effects, including liver toxicity, and should only be used under the guidance of a healthcare professional.

Magnolia Bark

Magnolia bark is a plant that has been used in traditional Chinese medicine for centuries for its calming effects. It contains compounds that interact with the brain's GABA receptors, which help to promote relaxation and reduce anxiety. Magnolia bark has been shown to improve sleep quality and reduce the time it takes to fall asleep. It is available in many forms, including teas, capsules, and tinctures.

California Poppy

California poppy is a plant that has been used for centuries for its calming and sedative effects. It contains compounds that interact with the brain's GABA receptors, which help to promote relaxation and reduce anxiety. California poppy has been shown to improve sleep quality and reduce the time it takes to fall asleep. It is available in many forms, including teas, capsules, and tinctures.

Hops

Hops is a plant that is commonly used in brewing beer, but it also has sedative effects. It contains compounds that interact with the brain's GABA receptors, which help to promote relaxation and reduce anxiety. Hops has been shown to improve sleep quality and reduce the time it takes to fall asleep. It is available in many forms, including teas, capsules, and tinctures.

Melatonin

Melatonin is a hormone that is naturally produced by the body to regulate sleep-wake cycles. It can also be taken as a supplement to help promote sleep. Melatonin has been shown to improve sleep quality and reduce the time it takes to fall asleep. It is available in many forms, including tablets, capsules, and tinctures.

Conclusion

Herbal remedies offer a natural and safe alternative for promoting better sleep. Valerian root, chamomile, passionflower, lavender, lemon balm, ashwagandha, skullcap, kava, magnolia bark, California poppy, hops, and melatonin are just some of the herbs and supplements that have been shown to improve sleep quality and reduce the time it takes to fall asleep. However, it's important to note that not all herbal remedies are safe for everyone and some may interact with medications. It's always best to consult with a healthcare professional before using any herbal remedy for sleep issues.

Homeopathic remedies for stress and fatigue

Stress and fatigue are two common ailments that are prevalent in our modern society. Stress is caused by various factors such as work, relationships, finances, and health, and can manifest in physical and emotional symptoms such as anxiety, irritability, and insomnia. Fatigue, on the other hand, is characterized by feelings of exhaustion and weakness, and can be caused by a range of factors such as poor sleep, poor diet, and chronic health conditions. In this chapter, we will explore the use of homeopathic remedies for stress and fatigue, including their benefits, how they work, and which remedies are most effective.

What is Homeopathy?

Homeopathy is a system of medicine that is based on the principle of "like cures like." This means that a substance that causes a symptom in a healthy person can be used to treat the same symptom in a sick person. Homeopathic remedies are made from natural substances such as plants, minerals, and animal products, and are diluted to the point where only trace amounts of the original substance remain. The remedies are believed to work by stimulating the body's natural healing mechanisms.

Benefits of Homeopathic Remedies for Stress and Fatigue:

Homeopathic remedies for stress and fatigue offer several benefits over conventional medicine. First, they are safe and non-toxic, with few side effects. Second, they are gentle and non-invasive, making them suitable for people of all ages and health conditions. Third, they work on a holistic level, treating the whole person rather than just the symptoms. Finally, they are often more affordable than conventional medicine, making them accessible to a wider range of people.

How Homeopathic Remedies Work for Stress and Fatigue:

Homeopathic remedies work by stimulating the body's natural healing mechanisms. They are believed to work on a deep level, treating the underlying causes of stress and fatigue rather than just the symptoms. Homeopathic remedies for stress and fatigue are chosen based on the individual's specific symptoms, as well as their emotional and mental state. The remedies are then diluted to the appropriate potency and administered in small doses.

Top Homeopathic Remedies for Stress and Fatigue:

Kali Phosphoricum: This remedy is indicated for mental and physical fatigue, as well as nervous exhaustion. It is also useful for people who feel weak and run down due to overwork or stress.

Nux Vomica: This remedy is indicated for people who are irritable and oversensitive to noise and light. It is also useful for people who have trouble sleeping due to an overactive mind.

Gelsemium: This remedy is indicated for people who feel weak and lethargic due to stress and anxiety. It is also useful for people who experience trembling or weakness in the limbs.

Ignatia: This remedy is indicated for people who are emotionally sensitive and prone to mood swings. It is also useful for people who experience fatigue as a result of grief or emotional stress.

Arsenicum Album: This remedy is indicated for people who are anxious and fearful, and who experience restlessness and insomnia as a result. It is also useful for people who experience physical weakness and exhaustion.

Phosphoric Acid: This remedy is indicated for people who experience mental and physical exhaustion as a result of grief, loss, or emotional stress.

Sepia: This remedy is indicated for people who feel exhausted and overwhelmed due to the demands of work and family. It is also useful for women who experience fatigue and mood swings due to hormonal imbalances.

Dosage and Administration of Homeopathic Remedies:

Homeopathic remedies for stress and fatigue are typically taken in small doses, either in the form of pellets, drops, or tablets. The dosage and administration of the remedies will depend on the individual's specific symptoms and the potency of the remedy. It is important to follow the instructions on the label or consult with a homeopathic practitioner for guidance.

In general, homeopathic remedies are taken orally and should be taken on an empty stomach, at least 30 minutes before or after eating or drinking. The remedy should be allowed to dissolve under the tongue or in the mouth, and should not be swallowed whole. The frequency of dosing will depend on the individual's symptoms and the potency of the remedy. Some remedies may need to be taken several times a day, while others may only need to be taken once a week or less.

It is important to note that homeopathic remedies should not be used as a substitute for conventional medical care. If you are experiencing severe or chronic symptoms of stress or fatigue, it is important to consult with a healthcare professional to determine the underlying cause and to develop a comprehensive treatment plan.

Conclusion:

Homeopathic remedies offer a safe, gentle, and effective way to treat stress and fatigue. They work by stimulating the body's natural healing mechanisms, and are chosen based on the individual's specific symptoms and emotional and mental state. The remedies are safe and non-toxic, and offer several benefits over conventional medicine. If you are experiencing symptoms of stress or fatigue, consider exploring the use of homeopathic remedies with the guidance of a homeopathic practitioner.

Promoting Healthy Skin

Natural remedies for acne, eczema, and psoriasis

Acne, eczema, and psoriasis are three common skin conditions that affect millions of people worldwide. While there are many conventional treatments available for these conditions, natural remedies are often preferred due to their effectiveness and lack of side effects. This chapter will discuss some of the most effective natural remedies for acne, eczema, and psoriasis.

Acne:

Acne is a skin condition that occurs when hair follicles become clogged with oil and dead skin cells. This can lead to pimples, blackheads, and whiteheads. Here are some natural remedies for acne:

Tea tree oil: Tea tree oil has anti-inflammatory and antimicrobial properties, making it an effective treatment for acne. Apply a few drops of tea tree oil to a cotton swab and dab it onto the affected area.

Aloe vera: Aloe vera has anti-inflammatory and antibacterial properties, making it an effective treatment for acne. Apply aloe vera gel directly to the affected area.

Zinc: Zinc is an essential mineral that can help reduce inflammation and acne. You can take zinc supplements or eat foods that are high in zinc, such as oysters, beef, and pumpkin seeds.

Green tea: Green tea has anti-inflammatory properties and can help reduce acne. You can drink green tea or apply it topically to the affected area.

Honey: Honey has antibacterial properties and can help reduce acne. Apply a thin layer of honey to the affected area and leave it on for 10-15 minutes before rinsing it off with warm water.

Eczema:

Eczema is a skin condition that causes itching, inflammation, and redness. Here are some natural remedies for eczema:

Coconut oil: Coconut oil has anti-inflammatory and moisturizing properties, making it an effective treatment for eczema. Apply coconut oil to the affected area and massage it in.

Oatmeal: Oatmeal has anti-inflammatory properties and can help soothe eczema. Add oatmeal to your bathwater or make an oatmeal paste and apply it directly to the affected area.

Apple cider vinegar: Apple cider vinegar has anti-inflammatory properties and can help reduce itching and inflammation associated with eczema. Dilute apple cider vinegar with water and apply it to the affected area.

Turmeric: Turmeric has anti-inflammatory properties and can help reduce itching and inflammation associated with eczema. Mix turmeric with coconut oil and apply it to the affected area.

Chamomile: Chamomile has anti-inflammatory properties and can help soothe eczema. Brew chamomile tea and apply it to the affected area with a cotton swab.

Psoriasis:

Psoriasis is a skin condition that causes dry, red, and scaly patches on the skin. Here are some natural remedies for psoriasis:

Fish oil: Fish oil contains omega-3 fatty acids, which have anti-inflammatory properties and can help reduce psoriasis. Take fish oil supplements or eat foods that are high in omega-3 fatty acids, such as salmon and sardines.

Aloe vera: Aloe vera has anti-inflammatory and moisturizing properties, making it an effective treatment for psoriasis. Apply aloe vera gel directly to the affected area.

Dead sea salt: Dead sea salt has anti-inflammatory properties and can help reduce psoriasis. Add dead sea salt to your bathwater and soak in it for 15-20 minutes.

Turmeric: Turmeric has anti-inflammatory properties and can help reduce inflammation associated with psoriasis. Mix turmeric with coconut oil and apply it to the affected area.

Oregon grape: Oregon grape has anti-inflammatory properties and can help reduce inflammation associated with psoriasis. Apply Oregon grape cream or ointment directly to the affected area.

Vitamin D: Vitamin D can help reduce inflammation and improve skin health. You can take vitamin D supplements or get more vitamin D by spending time in the sun.

Probiotics: Probiotics can help improve gut health, which can reduce inflammation and improve psoriasis. You can take probiotic supplements or eat foods that are high in probiotics, such as yogurt and kefir.

Mahonia aquifolium: Mahonia aquifolium, also known as Oregon grape, has been shown to be an effective treatment for psoriasis. Apply a cream or ointment containing Mahonia aquifolium directly to the affected area.

Conclusion:

Acne, eczema, and psoriasis are common skin conditions that can be treated with natural remedies. Tea tree oil, aloe vera, zinc, green tea, and honey are effective treatments for acne. Coconut oil, oatmeal, apple cider vinegar, turmeric, and chamomile can help soothe eczema. Fish oil, aloe vera, dead sea salt, turmeric, Oregon grape, vitamin D, and probiotics can help improve psoriasis. While natural remedies can be effective, it's important to consult with a healthcare provider before trying any new treatments.

Herbal remedies for dry skin and wrinkles

Herbal remedies are becoming increasingly popular for treating a wide range of health problems, including dry skin and wrinkles.

These remedies can be very effective and are often less expensive than commercial products. In this chapter, we will explore some of the best herbal remedies for dry skin and wrinkles, and how to use them effectively.

Understanding Dry Skin and Wrinkles:

Dry skin is a common condition that occurs when the skin loses moisture. This can cause the skin to become tight, itchy, and flaky. Dry skin can be caused by a variety of factors, including aging, weather changes, and certain medical conditions.

Wrinkles are another common skin problem, particularly as we age. Wrinkles are caused by a combination of factors, including genetics, sun exposure, smoking, and natural aging.

Herbal Remedies for Dry Skin and Wrinkles:

Aloe Vera:
Aloe vera is an excellent remedy for dry skin and wrinkles. It contains anti-inflammatory and moisturizing properties that can help soothe and hydrate dry skin. Aloe vera also contains antioxidants that can help reduce the appearance of wrinkles.

To use aloe vera, simply apply the gel from the plant directly to the affected area. You can also use aloe vera products that contain high levels of aloe vera.

Calendula:
Calendula is a gentle herb that is ideal for soothing dry, irritated skin. It contains anti-inflammatory properties that can help reduce inflammation and redness, and it can also help to hydrate the skin.

To use calendula, you can make a tea by steeping the dried herb in hot water for 10-15 minutes. You can then apply the cooled tea to the affected area with a cotton ball.

Chamomile:
Chamomile is another gentle herb that can help soothe dry skin. It contains anti-inflammatory and antioxidant properties that can help to reduce inflammation and protect the skin from damage.

To use chamomile, you can make a tea by steeping the dried herb in hot water for 10-15 minutes. You can then apply the cooled tea to the affected area with a cotton ball.

Coconut Oil:
Coconut oil is a natural moisturizer that can help hydrate dry skin. It contains medium-chain fatty acids that can penetrate the skin easily, and it also contains antioxidants that can help to protect the skin from damage.

To use coconut oil, simply apply a small amount to the affected area and massage it into the skin.

Green Tea:
Green tea is an excellent source of antioxidants, which can help to protect the skin from damage and reduce the appearance of wrinkles. Green tea also contains anti-inflammatory properties that can help to reduce inflammation and redness.

To use green tea, you can make a tea by steeping the tea leaves in hot water for 10-15 minutes. You can then apply the cooled tea to the affected area with a cotton ball.

Rosehip Oil:
Rosehip oil is a natural source of vitamin A and vitamin C, which can help to reduce the appearance of wrinkles and promote healthy skin. It also contains essential fatty acids that can help to hydrate the skin.

To use rosehip oil, simply apply a small amount to the affected area and massage it into the skin.

Shea Butter:
Shea butter is a natural moisturizer that can help to hydrate dry skin. It contains essential fatty acids and vitamins A and E, which can help to nourish the skin and protect it from damage.

To use shea butter, simply apply a small amount to the affected area and massage it into the skin.

It's also important to maintain a healthy lifestyle to support healthy skin. This includes eating a balanced diet rich in vitamins and minerals, staying hydrated by drinking plenty of water, getting regular exercise, and avoiding smoking and excessive sun exposure.

In addition to these herbal remedies, there are also other natural remedies that can help with dry skin and wrinkles, such as staying hydrated, using gentle skincare products, and avoiding harsh soaps and detergents. By taking care of your skin both internally and externally, you can help to promote healthy, glowing skin and reduce the appearance of wrinkles.

In conclusion, herbal remedies can be a great way to treat dry skin and wrinkles. There are many different herbs and oils that can be effective for hydrating and nourishing the skin, reducing inflammation and redness, and promoting healthy, youthful skin. With a little experimentation and some patience, you can find the right herbal remedies to help keep your skin looking and feeling its best.

How to make your own natural skincare products

Natural skincare products have become increasingly popular in recent years as people become more conscious of the chemicals and synthetic ingredients in many commercial products. Making your own natural skincare products at home is not only cost-effective, but it also allows you to control the ingredients that go into your products. This chapter will guide you through the steps to make your own natural skincare products.

Step 1: Gather Ingredients and Supplies

The first step in making your own natural skincare products is to gather the necessary ingredients and supplies. The following are some ingredients commonly used in natural skincare products:

Carrier oils (such as coconut oil, jojoba oil, and olive oil)
Essential oils (such as lavender, tea tree, and peppermint)
Beeswax

Shea butter

Aloe vera gel

Raw honey

Bentonite clay

Vitamin E oil

Vegetable glycerin

Herbal extracts (such as chamomile, calendula, and lavender)

In addition to ingredients, you will need some supplies to make your natural skincare products. These may include:

Mixing bowls

Measuring cups and spoons

Whisk or handheld mixer

Double boiler or saucepan

Glass jars or containers for storage

Step 2: Choose the Right Ingredients for Your Skin Type

Before you start making your natural skincare products, it's important to understand your skin type and choose ingredients that will work best for you. The following are some general guidelines for choosing ingredients based on skin type:

Dry Skin: Choose ingredients that are moisturizing and nourishing, such as shea butter, avocado oil, and aloe vera gel.

Oily Skin: Choose ingredients that are light and non-comedogenic, such as jojoba oil, grapeseed oil, and witch hazel.

Combination Skin: Choose ingredients that balance oily and dry areas of the skin, such as argan oil, chamomile extract, and green tea extract.

Sensitive Skin: Choose ingredients that are gentle and non-irritating, such as chamomile oil, oatmeal, and honey.

Step 3: Create Your Recipes

Once you have gathered your ingredients and chosen the ones that are right for your skin type, it's time to create your recipes. The following are some simple recipes for natural skincare products that you can make at home.

Recipe 1: Homemade Lip Balm

Ingredients:

2 tablespoons beeswax

2 tablespoons shea butter

2 tablespoons coconut oil

10-15 drops of essential oil (such as peppermint or lavender)

Directions:

Melt the beeswax, shea butter, and coconut oil in a double boiler or saucepan over low heat.

Remove from heat and stir in the essential oil.

Pour the mixture into small containers (such as lip balm tubes or tins) and let cool and solidify.

Recipe 2: Soothing Face Mask

Ingredients:

1 tablespoon bentonite clay

1 tablespoon raw honey

1 tablespoon aloe vera gel

3-4 drops of lavender essential oil

Directions:

Mix all the ingredients together in a bowl until well combined.

Apply the mixture to your face and let sit for 10-15 minutes.

Rinse off with warm water and pat dry.

Recipe 3: Nourishing Body Butter

Ingredients:

1 cup shea butter

1/2 cup coconut oil

1/4 cup jojoba oil

10-15 drops of essential oil (such as vanilla or lavender)

Directions:

Melt the shea butter, coconut oil, and jojoba oil in a double boiler or saucepan over low heat.

2. Remove from heat and stir in the essential oil.

Transfer the mixture to a bowl and let it cool for 10-15 minutes.

Use a handheld mixer or whisk to whip the mixture until it becomes light and fluffy.

Transfer the body butter to a jar or container and store at room temperature.

Recipe 4: Refreshing Facial Toner

Ingredients:

1/2 cup distilled water

1/4 cup witch hazel

1/4 cup rose water

5 drops of tea tree essential oil

Directions:

Combine all the ingredients in a bottle and shake well to mix.

Apply the toner to a cotton pad and swipe it over your face after cleansing.

Store the toner in the refrigerator for a cooling and refreshing effect.

Step 4: Store and Use Your Natural Skincare Products

After making your natural skincare products, it's important to store them properly to maintain their effectiveness and prevent spoilage. Store your products in a cool, dark place away from direct sunlight and heat.

To use your natural skincare products, follow these general guidelines:

Apply a small amount of the product to your skin and massage it in gently.

Start with a patch test before using a new product to make sure you don't have any allergic reactions.

Use the products within 3-6 months to ensure freshness and effectiveness.

Conclusion:

Making your own natural skincare products can be a fun and rewarding experience. By using high-quality, natural ingredients, you can create products that are tailored to your specific skin type and needs. Whether you're looking for a soothing face mask or a nourishing body butter, these simple recipes can help you get started on your natural skincare journey. Remember to always patch test new products and store them properly to ensure their effectiveness and safety.

Natural Remedies for Women's Health Issues

Natural remedies for PMS and menstrual cramps

Premenstrual syndrome (PMS) and menstrual cramps are common issues that women face during their menstrual cycle. PMS symptoms can include bloating, mood swings, breast tenderness, fatigue, and irritability. Menstrual cramps, on the other hand, can be mild or severe and can cause discomfort, pain, and even disrupt daily activities.

While many over-the-counter medications can provide relief for PMS and menstrual cramps, natural remedies are an effective alternative that can be used to alleviate symptoms and provide relief. Here are some natural remedies that you can use to help ease PMS and menstrual cramps.

Exercise

Physical activity can help reduce the severity of PMS symptoms and alleviate menstrual cramps. Regular exercise can improve blood flow and help release endorphins, which are natural painkillers. Activities such as yoga, walking, and swimming can also help reduce stress and improve overall well-being.

Heat Therapy

Applying heat to the lower abdomen can help relieve menstrual cramps. You can use a heating pad or a hot water bottle to apply heat to the affected area. Taking a warm bath or shower can also help relax your muscles and alleviate cramps.

Ginger

Ginger has anti-inflammatory properties and can help reduce inflammation and pain associated with menstrual cramps. You can consume ginger in various forms, including ginger tea, ginger supplements, or adding fresh ginger to your meals.

Magnesium

Magnesium is a mineral that can help reduce menstrual cramps. It helps relax muscles and alleviate pain by reducing the levels of prostaglandins, which are hormone-like substances that cause inflammation and pain. Foods high in magnesium include almonds, spinach, avocados, and dark chocolate. You can also take magnesium supplements after consulting with your doctor.

Chamomile Tea

Chamomile tea has anti-inflammatory properties and can help reduce menstrual cramps. It also has a calming effect that can help alleviate PMS symptoms, such as irritability and anxiety.

Omega-3 Fatty Acids

Omega-3 fatty acids can help reduce inflammation and alleviate menstrual cramps. Foods rich in omega-3 fatty acids include fatty fish such as salmon and mackerel, flaxseed, chia seeds, and walnuts. You can also take omega-3 supplements after consulting with your doctor.

Vitamin B6

Vitamin B6 can help alleviate PMS symptoms such as mood swings, depression, and irritability. It can also help reduce water retention and bloating. Foods rich in vitamin B6 include bananas, spinach, and chickpeas. You can also take vitamin B6 supplements after consulting with your doctor.

Acupuncture

Acupuncture involves the insertion of fine needles into specific points in the body to help alleviate pain and promote healing. Studies have shown that acupuncture can help reduce menstrual cramps and other PMS symptoms.

Massage

Massaging the lower abdomen can help alleviate menstrual cramps by improving blood flow and reducing tension. You can use essential oils such as lavender or peppermint to enhance the relaxing effects of the massage.

Probiotics

Probiotics are beneficial bacteria that can help improve gut health and reduce inflammation. They can also help alleviate PMS symptoms such as bloating and constipation. You can consume probiotics in the form of supplements or by consuming fermented foods such as yogurt, kefir, and sauerkraut.

it is important to note that not all natural remedies work for everyone, and it is essential to consult with your healthcare provider before trying any new remedy. Additionally, if you experience severe menstrual cramps or heavy bleeding, it is important to seek medical attention as it may be a sign of an underlying medical condition.

It is also important to maintain a healthy lifestyle, including a balanced diet and regular exercise, to help reduce the severity of PMS symptoms and menstrual cramps. Avoiding caffeine, alcohol, and processed foods can also help alleviate symptoms.

In summary, natural remedies can be an effective alternative to traditional medication for alleviating PMS symptoms and menstrual cramps. Incorporating these remedies into your routine, along with a healthy lifestyle, can help reduce the severity of symptoms and improve overall well-being. However, it is important to consult with your healthcare provider before trying any new remedy to ensure it is safe and effective for you.

Herbal remedies for menopause symptoms

Menopause is a natural biological process that marks the end of reproductive years for women. It usually occurs between the ages of 45 and 55, and is characterized by a decrease in estrogen production by the ovaries. This hormonal shift can cause a range of physical and emotional symptoms that can be quite uncomfortable and disruptive to a woman's daily life. While hormone replacement therapy (HRT) is often used to manage menopause symptoms, it's not always the best option for everyone. Some women prefer to use herbal remedies to ease their symptoms. In this chapter, we'll take a closer look at some of the most effective herbal remedies for menopause symptoms.

Black Cohosh

Black cohosh (Actaea racemosa) is a popular herbal remedy for menopause symptoms. It's been used for centuries by Native Americans to treat a range of women's health issues. Black cohosh is believed to work by mimicking the effects of estrogen in the body. This can help alleviate symptoms such as hot flashes, mood swings, and vaginal dryness. Some studies have found that black cohosh can also help reduce bone loss in postmenopausal women.

There are a number of different forms of black cohosh available, including capsules, tablets, and liquid extracts. The recommended dose varies depending on the form, so it's important to follow the instructions on the product label. Some people may experience mild side effects when taking black cohosh, such as stomach upset or headaches. It's also important to note that black cohosh may interact with certain medications, so it's important to talk to your doctor before taking this herb.

Red Clover

Red clover (Trifolium pratense) is another herb that's often used to ease menopause symptoms. Like black cohosh, red clover contains compounds that are similar to estrogen. This can help reduce hot flashes and other symptoms of menopause. Red clover may also have a protective effect on bone health, which is particularly important for postmenopausal women who are at increased risk of osteoporosis.

Red clover is available in various forms, including teas, capsules, and tinctures. It's generally considered safe for most people, but it can interact with certain medications, such as blood thinners. If you're taking any medications, it's a good idea to talk to your doctor before taking red clover.

Soy

Soy is a popular dietary supplement that's often recommended for menopausal women. Soy contains compounds called phytoestrogens, which are similar to estrogen. This can help reduce hot flashes and other symptoms of menopause. Soy may also have a protective effect on bone health.

Soy is available in various forms, including soy milk, tofu, and soy supplements. Some women find that drinking soy milk or eating tofu can help ease their symptoms. Soy supplements are also available, but it's important to choose a high-quality product and follow the recommended dose.

Dong Quai

Dong quai (Angelica sinensis) is a traditional Chinese herb that's often used to treat menopause symptoms. Dong quai is believed to work by balancing the body's hormonal systems. This can help alleviate symptoms such as hot flashes, vaginal dryness, and mood swings.

Dong quai is available in various forms, including teas, capsules, and tinctures. It's generally considered safe for most people, but it can interact with certain medications, such as blood thinners. If you're taking any medications, it's a good idea to talk to your doctor before taking dong quai.

Ginseng

Ginseng is a popular herbal remedy that's often used to improve energy and reduce stress. Some studies have also found that ginseng can help reduce menopause symptoms, such as hot flashes and mood swings. Ginseng is believed to work by regulating the body's hormonal systems.

Ginseng is available in various forms, including teas, capsules, and tinctures. It's generally considered safe for most people, but it can interact with certain medications, such as blood thinners and blood pressure medications. If you're taking any medications, it's a good idea to talk to your doctor before taking ginseng.

St. John's Wort

St. John's Wort (Hypericum perforatum) is an herb that's often used to treat depression and anxiety. Some studies have also found that it may be helpful for reducing hot flashes and other menopause symptoms. St. John's Wort is believed to work by increasing the levels of serotonin and other neurotransmitters in the brain.

St. John's Wort is available in various forms, including capsules, tablets, and tinctures. It's generally considered safe for most people, but it can interact with certain medications, such as antidepressants and birth control pills. If you're taking any medications, it's a good idea to talk to your doctor before taking St. John's Wort.

Evening Primrose Oil

Evening primrose oil (Oenothera biennis) is an oil that's extracted from the seeds of the evening primrose plant. It's often used to reduce inflammation and improve skin health, but it may also be helpful for reducing menopause symptoms. Evening primrose oil is believed to work by increasing the levels of prostaglandins in the body, which can help regulate hormonal systems.

Evening primrose oil is available in various forms, including capsules and oil. It's generally considered safe for most people, but it can interact with certain medications, such as blood thinners. If you're taking any medications, it's a good idea to talk to your doctor before taking evening primrose oil.

Other Herbal Remedies

In addition to the herbs mentioned above, there are several other herbs that may be helpful for reducing menopause symptoms. These include:

Chaste tree berry (Vitex agnus-castus): This herb is often used to regulate menstrual cycles and reduce hot flashes.
Sage (Salvia officinalis): Sage is believed to have a cooling effect on the body, which can help reduce hot flashes.
Licorice root (Glycyrrhiza glabra): Licorice root may help reduce hot flashes and other menopause symptoms by regulating hormonal systems.
It's important to note that herbal remedies are not regulated by the FDA in the same way that prescription drugs are. This means that the quality and purity of herbal supplements can vary widely. It's important to choose a high-quality product from a reputable manufacturer. It's also important to talk to your doctor before taking any herbal remedies, especially if you're taking any medications or have any medical conditions.

In addition to herbal remedies, there are other natural approaches that can help manage menopause symptoms. These include:

Lifestyle changes: Eating a healthy diet, exercising regularly, and getting enough sleep can all help reduce menopause symptoms. Avoiding triggers such as spicy foods and hot drinks can also help reduce hot flashes.

Mind-body therapies: Practices such as yoga, meditation, and acupuncture can help reduce stress and improve overall well-being, which can in turn help reduce menopause symptoms.

Alternative therapies: Some women find relief from menopause symptoms by using alternative therapies such as chiropractic care, massage therapy, or biofeedback.

It's important to remember that menopause is a natural process, and it's not a disease that needs to be cured. However, the symptoms of menopause can be uncomfortable and disruptive, and it's important to find ways to manage them that work for you. Herbal remedies and other natural approaches can be a safe and effective way to manage menopause symptoms, but it's important to talk to your doctor before trying any new treatments. With the right approach, you can navigate this transition with grace and ease.

How to support reproductive health naturally

Reproductive health is essential for both men and women to maintain a healthy and happy life. However, factors such as stress, pollution, and unhealthy lifestyles can affect reproductive health, leading to issues such as infertility, irregular periods, and low sperm count. While there are medical treatments available, many people prefer natural remedies to support their reproductive health. In this chapter, we will explore various ways to support reproductive health naturally.

Eat a healthy diet

A healthy diet is essential for reproductive health. Eating a diet rich in fruits, vegetables, and whole grains provides the body with the necessary nutrients for reproductive health. Include foods that are high in vitamin C, such as citrus fruits, strawberries, and broccoli, as this vitamin helps improve sperm count and motility in men and reduce the risk of ovarian cancer in women. Foods rich in vitamin E, such as nuts, seeds, and spinach, can also improve fertility in both men and women.

Exercise regularly

Regular exercise is crucial for reproductive health. It helps regulate hormone levels, reduce stress, and improve blood flow to the reproductive organs. Exercise also promotes weight loss, which can improve fertility in overweight individuals. Engage in moderate exercise such as walking, swimming, or yoga for at least 30 minutes a day, five times a week.

Manage stress

Stress can adversely affect reproductive health. Chronic stress can disrupt hormone levels and interfere with ovulation and sperm production. Therefore, it is essential to manage stress through relaxation techniques such as meditation, deep breathing, and yoga.

Avoid toxins

Toxins such as tobacco smoke, alcohol, and environmental pollutants can harm reproductive health. Smoking has been linked to decreased fertility in both men and women, while excessive alcohol consumption can lower testosterone levels in men and disrupt menstrual cycles in women. Limit exposure to environmental toxins by avoiding products that contain harmful chemicals such as pesticides and cleaning products.

Get enough sleep

Sleep is essential for overall health and wellbeing, including reproductive health. Lack of sleep can lead to imbalanced hormone levels, decreased libido, and reduced fertility. Aim for at least seven to eight hours of sleep per night and establish a consistent sleep routine.

Try herbal remedies

Various herbs are believed to support reproductive health. For instance, maca root is known to improve libido and sperm count in men and reduce menopausal symptoms in women. Tribulus terrestris is also believed to enhance fertility in men and women. However, it is essential to consult with a healthcare provider before using herbal remedies, as some can interact with medications or cause side effects.

Consider supplements

Supplements such as folic acid, vitamin D, and omega-3 fatty acids are known to improve reproductive health. Folic acid is essential for women trying to conceive, as it can prevent birth defects. Vitamin D is crucial for male fertility, and low levels of this vitamin have been linked to reduced sperm count and motility. Omega-3 fatty acids can improve sperm quality and reduce the risk of miscarriage in women.

Practice safe sex

Practicing safe sex is crucial for preventing sexually transmitted infections (STIs), which can affect reproductive health. Always use condoms during sexual activity, especially if you are not in a monogamous relationship.

Additionally, it is crucial to maintain open communication with your healthcare provider about any concerns or changes in your reproductive health. Regular check-ups and screenings can also help detect and prevent any potential issues.

In conclusion, natural remedies can support reproductive health, but it is essential to make lifestyle changes and seek professional guidance when necessary. With the right care and attention, you can maintain optimal reproductive health and improve your chances of a happy and healthy life.

Natural Remedies for Children's Health

Natural remedies for ear infections and colds in children

As a parent, you want nothing but the best for your child's health. However, ear infections and colds are common ailments that children often experience. Instead of relying on over-the-counter medicines, natural remedies can be used to ease symptoms and help your child feel better. In this chapter, we will discuss natural remedies for ear infections and colds in children.

Natural Remedies for Ear Infections:

Garlic Oil Drops: Garlic has natural antibacterial properties and can be used to treat ear infections. Crush a few garlic cloves and mix them with olive oil. Heat the mixture for a few minutes, then strain the oil and cool it. Apply a few drops of this oil into the ear canal, and your child should feel better within a few hours.

Warm Compress: A warm compress can help relieve the pain associated with an ear infection. Soak a washcloth in warm water, squeeze out the excess water, and place it on the affected ear. Leave it on for a few minutes, and repeat the process several times a day.

Tea Tree Oil: Tea tree oil has antiseptic properties and can be used to treat ear infections. Mix a few drops of tea tree oil with olive oil, and apply it to the outer ear. Repeat the process several times a day.

Breast Milk: Breast milk has natural antibodies and can be used to treat ear infections. Put a few drops of breast milk into the infected ear, and your child should feel better within a few hours.

Natural Remedies for Colds:

Honey: Honey has natural antibacterial and antiviral properties and can be used to treat colds. Mix a teaspoon of honey with warm water, and give it to your child several times a day.

Salt Water Gargle: Gargling with salt water can help relieve the symptoms of a cold. Mix a teaspoon of salt with warm water and have your child gargle with it several times a day.

Eucalyptus Oil: Eucalyptus oil has antiviral properties and can be used to treat colds. Mix a few drops of eucalyptus oil with warm water, and have your child inhale the steam.

Chicken Soup: Chicken soup has anti-inflammatory properties and can be used to treat colds. Make a homemade chicken soup and give it to your child several times a day.

Here are some additional natural remedies for ear infections and colds in children:

Mullein Oil: Mullein oil has anti-inflammatory properties and can be used to soothe ear infections. Warm up a few drops of mullein oil and put it into the affected ear. Gently massage the outer ear to help the oil work its way into the ear canal. Repeat this process a few times a day.

Probiotics: Probiotics are beneficial bacteria that can help boost your child's immune system and fight off infections. You can find probiotics in yogurt, kefir, and other fermented foods. You can also give your child probiotic supplements.

Ginger: Ginger has anti-inflammatory and antiviral properties and can help relieve cold symptoms. You can make ginger tea by boiling ginger slices in water and adding honey to taste. You can also add ginger to soups and other dishes.

Vitamin C: Vitamin C is an antioxidant that can help boost your child's immune system and fight off infections. You can give your child vitamin C supplements or increase their intake of vitamin C-rich foods such as citrus fruits, strawberries, and broccoli.

Rest: One of the most important things you can do to help your child recover from an ear infection or cold is to ensure that they get plenty of rest. Make sure your child gets enough sleep and avoid over-scheduling them with activities.

It is important to note that natural remedies should not replace medical treatment. If your child's symptoms are severe or do not improve after a few days, you should seek medical attention from a healthcare provider. Additionally, some natural remedies may not be suitable for all children, so it is important to consult with a healthcare provider before trying any new remedies.

Herbal remedies for ADHD and anxiety in children

Attention deficit hyperactivity disorder (ADHD) and anxiety are two common mental health conditions that affect children. ADHD is characterized by symptoms such as inattention, hyperactivity, and impulsivity. Anxiety, on the other hand, involves feelings of fear and worry that can interfere with daily activities. While medication is commonly prescribed to manage these conditions, some parents are turning to herbal remedies as an alternative or complementary treatment. This chapter will explore the effectiveness and safety of herbal remedies for ADHD and anxiety in children.

Herbal Remedies for ADHD:

Ginkgo Biloba:
Ginkgo biloba is an herb that has been used for centuries in traditional medicine. It is believed to improve cognitive function, memory, and concentration. Some studies have suggested that ginkgo biloba may be effective in reducing ADHD symptoms, such as inattention and impulsivity. However, more research is needed to confirm its effectiveness and safety for children.

Bacopa Monnieri:
Bacopa monnieri, also known as Brahmi, is an herb commonly used in Ayurvedic medicine. It is believed to enhance memory, cognitive function, and reduce anxiety. Some studies have shown that bacopa may be effective in reducing ADHD symptoms, such as hyperactivity and impulsivity. However, more research is needed to confirm its effectiveness and safety for children.

Rhodiola Rosea:
Rhodiola rosea is an adaptogenic herb that is believed to reduce stress and improve cognitive function. Some studies have

suggested that rhodiola may be effective in reducing ADHD symptoms, such as inattention and impulsivity. However, more research is needed to confirm its effectiveness and safety for children.

Pycnogenol:

Pycnogenol is a natural extract from the bark of the French maritime pine tree. It is believed to have antioxidant and anti-inflammatory properties. Some studies have suggested that pycnogenol may be effective in reducing ADHD symptoms, such as inattention and hyperactivity. However, more research is needed to confirm its effectiveness and safety for children.

Herbal Remedies for Anxiety:

Chamomile:

Chamomile is an herb that is commonly used to promote relaxation and reduce anxiety. It is believed to have a calming effect on the nervous system. Some studies have shown that chamomile may be effective in reducing anxiety symptoms in children. It is generally considered safe, but it can cause allergic reactions in some people.

Valerian Root:

Valerian root is an herb that is commonly used to promote relaxation and improve sleep. It is believed to have a calming effect on the nervous system. Some studies have shown that valerian may be effective in reducing anxiety symptoms in children. However, it can cause drowsiness and should not be used in combination with other sedative medications.

Passionflower:

Passionflower is an herb that is commonly used to promote relaxation and reduce anxiety. It is believed to have a calming effect on the nervous system. Some studies have shown that passionflower may be effective in reducing anxiety symptoms in children. However, it can cause drowsiness and should not be used in combination with other sedative medications.

Lavender:

Lavender is an herb that is commonly used to promote relaxation and reduce anxiety. It is believed to have a calming effect on the nervous system. Some studies have shown that lavender may be effective in reducing anxiety symptoms in children. It is generally considered safe, but it can cause allergic reactions in some people.

Safety and Precautions:

While herbal remedies are generally considered safe, it is important to use them with caution, especially when treating children. Some herbs can interact with medications or cause allergic reactions. It is important to consult a healthcare provider before using any herbal remedies, especially if your child is taking medication for ADHD or anxiety. Additionally, some herbs can cause side effects such as drowsiness, upset stomach, or changes in blood pressure. It is important to monitor your child's response to any herbal remedies and discontinue use if any adverse reactions occur.

Dosage is also an important consideration when using herbal remedies. Dosages can vary depending on the herb and the form in which it is taken. It is important to follow the recommended dosage instructions and not exceed the maximum recommended dose. Always read the labels and follow the instructions carefully.

Conclusion:

Herbal remedies can be a safe and effective alternative or complementary treatment for ADHD and anxiety in children. However, it is important to use them with caution and under the guidance of a healthcare provider. Some herbs may interact with medications or cause adverse reactions. Dosage is also an important consideration, and it is important to follow the recommended dosage instructions. While more research is needed to confirm the effectiveness and safety of some herbal remedies, they offer a promising avenue for managing ADHD and anxiety in children without the potential side effects of medication.

How to make natural remedies that are safe for kids

Natural remedies have been used for centuries to treat various ailments, and they can be a safe and effective alternative to traditional medicine. When it comes to children, it is essential to choose remedies that are safe and gentle. In this chapter, we will discuss the benefits of natural remedies, the precautions to take when treating children, and how to prepare for making your own natural remedies.

Benefits of Natural Remedies for Children

Natural remedies have several benefits for children. They are safe and gentle, and they do not have the side effects that traditional medicines can have. They are also affordable and readily available. Here are some of the benefits of natural remedies for children:

They are gentle: Natural remedies are gentle on children's bodies, and they do not have the harsh side effects that some traditional medicines can have.

They are safe: Natural remedies are safe for children because they do not contain synthetic chemicals that can harm their health.

They are affordable: Natural remedies are often less expensive than traditional medicines, making them a more accessible option for families.

They are effective: Natural remedies have been used for centuries to treat various ailments, and many have been proven to be effective.

Precautions When Treating Children with Natural Remedies

While natural remedies are safe, there are still some precautions that you should take when treating children. Here are some of the precautions to keep in mind:

Consult with a healthcare professional: Before using any natural remedies, it is essential to consult with a healthcare professional to ensure that they are safe for your child.

Be cautious with dosages: Natural remedies can be potent, so it is important to be cautious with dosages. Always follow the instructions carefully and do not exceed the recommended dose.

Test for allergies: Some children may be allergic to certain natural remedies, so it is essential to test for allergies before using them.

Keep remedies out of reach: Natural remedies should be kept out of reach of children to prevent accidental ingestion.

How to Prepare for Making Natural Remedies

Before making natural remedies, it is essential to prepare properly. Here are some steps you can take to prepare:

Research the remedies: Before making any natural remedies, research them thoroughly to ensure that they are safe and effective for your child's condition.

Gather ingredients: Once you have decided on the remedies, gather all the necessary ingredients. Make sure to purchase high-quality, organic ingredients whenever possible.

Follow instructions carefully: When making natural remedies, it is important to follow the instructions carefully to ensure that the remedies are effective and safe.

Store remedies properly: Natural remedies should be stored in a cool, dry place and labeled clearly. Make sure to keep them out of reach of children.

Safe and Effective Natural Remedies for Children

Here are some safe and effective natural remedies for children:

Honey: Honey is a natural cough suppressant and can be given to children over one year of age. It is also a natural antibiotic and can be used to treat minor cuts and burns.

Chamomile tea: Chamomile tea is a gentle sedative and can be given to children to help them sleep. It is also a natural anti-inflammatory and can be used to treat digestive issues.

Eucalyptus oil: Eucalyptus oil can be used to treat respiratory issues such as colds and coughs. It can be used as a steam inhalation or added to a diffuser.

Ginger: Ginger is a natural anti-inflammatory and can be used to treat digestive issues such as nausea and vomiting. It can be added to tea or used in cooking.

Lavender oil: Lavender oil is a natural relaxant and can be used to help children sleep. It can be added to a diffuser or diluted in a carrier oil and applied to the skin.

Aloe vera: Aloe vera is a natural moisturizer and can be used to soothe skin irritations such as sunburns and insect bites. It can be applied directly to the skin.

Calendula: Calendula is a natural anti-inflammatory and can be used to soothe skin irritations such as diaper rash. It can be used in a salve or cream.

Peppermint: Peppermint is a natural digestive aid and can be used to treat stomach aches and nausea. It can be added to tea or used in cooking.

Apple cider vinegar: Apple cider vinegar is a natural remedy for various ailments, including sore throats and digestive issues. It can be added to water or used in cooking.

Elderberry: Elderberry is a natural immune booster and can be used to prevent and treat colds and flu. It can be taken in syrup or gummy form.

Conclusion

Natural remedies can be safe and effective for children when used properly. It is essential to take precautions and consult with a healthcare professional before using any natural remedies. With the right preparation and knowledge, natural remedies can be a valuable tool in helping your child maintain optimal health and well-being.

Living a Natural Healing Lifestyle

How to create a natural and toxin-free home

Creating a natural and toxin-free home is essential for maintaining a healthy and safe environment for you and your family. By making some simple changes, you can improve the air quality, reduce exposure to harmful chemicals, and create a healthier living space. This chapter will guide you through the steps to create a natural and toxin-free home.

Step 1: Declutter Your Home

The first step to creating a natural and toxin-free home is to declutter your space. Removing unnecessary items will help to reduce the accumulation of dust, which can be a source of allergens and toxins. Start by going through your belongings and getting rid of items you no longer need or use. Donate, sell, or recycle these items, and only keep the things that are essential to you.

Step 2: Use Natural Cleaning Products

Conventional cleaning products are often loaded with harmful chemicals that can be harmful to your health. Switching to natural cleaning products is an easy way to reduce exposure to toxins. You can make your own cleaning solutions using natural ingredients such as vinegar, baking soda, and essential oils. Alternatively, look for natural cleaning products that are free from harmful chemicals such as phthalates, parabens, and triclosan.

Step 3: Use Natural Pest Control

Chemical pest control products can be toxic to humans and pets. There are many natural pest control methods that you can use instead. For example, you can use diatomaceous earth, which is a natural substance that is effective at killing insects. You can also use essential oils such as peppermint, eucalyptus, and lavender to repel insects.

Step 4: Choose Natural Building Materials

When building or renovating your home, choose natural building materials whenever possible. Natural materials such as wood, stone, and clay are non-toxic and sustainable. They also have a lower carbon footprint compared to synthetic materials such as plastic and PVC.

Step 5: Use Non-Toxic Paint

Conventional paints contain volatile organic compounds (VOCs), which can be harmful to your health. When painting your home, choose non-toxic paints that are free from VOCs. Look for natural paints made from plant-based ingredients such as clay, milk, and lime.

Step 6: Invest in Air Purifiers and Plants

Indoor air quality can be up to five times worse than outdoor air quality. Investing in air purifiers and plants is an excellent way to improve indoor air quality. Air purifiers can help to remove pollutants such as dust, pollen, and mold from the air. Plants are natural air purifiers and can help to absorb harmful chemicals such as formaldehyde and benzene.

Step 7: Use Natural Personal Care Products

Personal care products such as shampoo, soap, and lotion can contain harmful chemicals such as parabens, phthalates, and sodium lauryl sulfate. Switching to natural personal care products is an easy way to reduce exposure to these toxins. Look for products that are free from harmful chemicals and made from natural ingredients such as coconut oil, shea butter, and essential oils.

Step 8: Choose Natural Fabrics

When choosing fabrics for your home, choose natural fabrics such as cotton, linen, and wool. Synthetic fabrics such as polyester and nylon are made from petroleum-based products and can release harmful chemicals into the air. Natural fabrics are also more sustainable and biodegradable.

Step 9: Avoid Synthetic Fragrances

Synthetic fragrances are often found in cleaning products, air fresheners, and personal care products. They can contain hundreds of chemicals, many of which are harmful to your health. Instead of using synthetic fragrances, use essential oils to add natural scents to your home.

Step 10: Create a Healthy Home Environment

Creating a healthy home environment involves more on step 10: Create a Healthy Home Environment

To create a healthy home environment, consider the following tips:

Open your windows: Opening your windows is an easy way to improve indoor air quality. It can help to remove stale air and bring in fresh air from outside.

Control humidity levels: High humidity levels can lead to mold growth, which can be harmful to your health. Use a dehumidifier to control humidity levels and prevent mold growth.

Use natural lighting: Natural lighting is not only more energy-efficient, but it can also improve your mood and overall well-being. Consider using natural lighting instead of artificial lighting whenever possible.

Create a green space: Creating a green space in your home can help to improve air quality and reduce stress levels. Consider adding indoor plants or creating a small garden in your backyard.

Use natural bedding: Natural bedding such as organic cotton or wool can help to reduce exposure to harmful chemicals. Look for bedding that is certified organic to ensure that it is free from harmful chemicals.

Conclusion

Creating a natural and toxin-free home is essential for maintaining a healthy and safe environment for you and your family. By following these steps, you can reduce exposure to harmful chemicals and create a healthier living space. Start by decluttering your home and using natural cleaning products. When building or renovating your home, choose natural building materials and non-toxic paint. Invest in air purifiers and plants to improve indoor air quality, and use natural personal care products and fabrics. Finally, create a healthy home environment by opening your windows, controlling humidity levels, using natural lighting, creating a green space, and using natural bedding. With these simple changes, you can create a natural and toxin-free home that promotes your health and well-being.

Natural remedies for cleaning and disinfecting

In recent times, there has been an increase in the use of natural remedies for various health issues. This trend has extended to the cleaning and disinfecting of our living spaces. Natural remedies offer a safer and healthier alternative to commercial cleaning products that may contain harmful chemicals. In this chapter, we will explore natural remedies for cleaning and disinfecting.

Vinegar

Vinegar is a natural and effective cleaning agent that has been used for centuries. It is a versatile cleaner that can be used for a wide range of cleaning tasks, from cleaning windows to removing stains. Vinegar has antimicrobial properties that make it effective at killing bacteria, viruses, and mold. To use vinegar as a cleaning agent, mix equal parts water and vinegar in a spray bottle and use it to clean surfaces such as countertops, floors, and sinks.

Lemon Juice

Lemon juice is another natural cleaning agent that can be used to disinfect surfaces. It contains citric acid, which is a natural disinfectant. Lemon juice can be used to remove stains, clean kitchen countertops, and disinfect cutting boards. To use lemon juice as a cleaning agent, mix equal parts water and lemon juice in a spray bottle and use it to clean surfaces.

Baking Soda

Baking soda is a natural cleaning agent that can be used to remove stains and deodorize surfaces. It can be used to clean kitchen appliances, carpets, and bathroom surfaces. Baking soda is effective at removing dirt and grime, and it has antimicrobial properties that make it effective at killing bacteria. To use baking soda as a cleaning agent, mix it with water to form a paste and use it to clean surfaces.

Tea Tree Oil

Tea tree oil is a natural disinfectant that has been used for centuries to treat various health conditions. It has antimicrobial properties that make it effective at killing bacteria, viruses, and fungi. Tea tree oil can be used to clean surfaces such as countertops, floors, and bathroom fixtures. To use tea tree oil as a cleaning agent, mix a few drops with water in a spray bottle and use it to clean surfaces.

Hydrogen Peroxide

Hydrogen peroxide is a natural disinfectant that can be used to clean surfaces and kill bacteria. It is effective at removing stains and whitening surfaces. Hydrogen peroxide can be used to clean cutting boards, countertops, and bathroom surfaces. To use hydrogen peroxide as a cleaning agent, mix equal parts water and hydrogen peroxide in a spray bottle and use it to clean surfaces.

Essential Oils

Essential oils such as lavender, peppermint, and eucalyptus have antimicrobial properties that make them effective at killing bacteria and viruses. They can be used to clean surfaces such as countertops, floors, and bathroom fixtures. Essential oils can also be used to deodorize surfaces and provide a pleasant scent. To use essential oils as a cleaning agent, mix a few drops with water in a spray bottle and use it to clean surfaces.

Conclusion

Natural remedies offer a safer and healthier alternative to commercial cleaning products that may contain harmful chemicals. Vinegar, lemon juice, baking soda, tea tree oil, hydrogen peroxide, and essential oils are effective natural remedies for cleaning and disinfecting. These natural remedies are readily available, inexpensive, and easy to use. By using natural remedies to clean and disinfect our living spaces, we can create a healthier environment for ourselves and our families.

Tips for incorporating natural healing into your everyday routine

Natural healing has been practiced for centuries, and it's still popular today. Incorporating natural healing into your daily routine can provide a range of benefits for both physical and mental well-being. In this chapter, we'll explore tips for incorporating natural healing into your everyday routine.

Start your day with meditation or yoga
Meditation and yoga are excellent ways to start your day. They help to calm the mind and reduce stress levels, which can have a positive impact on your overall health. Meditation and yoga also improve flexibility, balance, and strength. If you're new to these practices, consider taking a class or finding a guided meditation online.

Drink plenty of water
Drinking plenty of water is essential for good health. Water helps to flush out toxins from your body, aids in digestion, and keeps your skin looking healthy. Aim to drink at least eight glasses of water a day. You can also add lemon or cucumber to your water for added flavor and health benefits.

Eat a balanced diet
Eating a balanced diet is crucial for natural healing. Include plenty of fresh fruits and vegetables in your diet, along with whole grains, lean protein, and healthy fats. Avoid processed foods and sugary drinks, as they can contribute to inflammation and other health issues.

Practice aromatherapy
Aromatherapy is the use of essential oils to improve your physical and mental well-being. Essential oils can be used in a diffuser, applied topically, or added to a bath. Lavender oil, for example, is known for its calming properties, while peppermint oil can help to alleviate headaches.

Get plenty of sleep
Getting enough sleep is essential for good health. It helps to reduce stress levels, improve mood, and boost the immune system. Aim to get seven to eight hours of sleep each night. If you have trouble sleeping, try incorporating relaxation techniques into your bedtime routine, such as meditation or a warm bath.

Practice gratitude
Practicing gratitude is a powerful way to improve your mental well-being. Take a few minutes each day to reflect on the things you're grateful for. This can be as simple as being thankful for a good cup of coffee or a beautiful sunset. Practicing gratitude can help to reduce stress levels and improve your overall outlook on life.

Use natural remedies for common ailments

There are many natural remedies that can be used to treat common ailments. For example, honey can be used to soothe a sore throat, while ginger can help to alleviate nausea. Before using any natural remedy, be sure to research it thoroughly and talk to your healthcare provider.

Incorporate exercise into your routine
Exercise is essential for good health. It helps to improve cardiovascular health, boost mood, and reduce stress levels. Find an exercise that you enjoy, whether it's running, cycling, or yoga, and make it a regular part of your routine.

Practice self-care
Self-care is an essential part of natural healing. Taking care of your body and mind can help to reduce stress levels and improve your overall well-being. This can be as simple as taking a bubble bath or reading a book. Find activities that you enjoy and make time for them regularly.

Connect with nature
Connecting with nature is an excellent way to improve your mental and physical well-being. Spend time outdoors, whether it's going for a hike or simply sitting in the park. This can help to reduce stress levels and improve your mood.

In conclusion, incorporating natural healing into your everyday routine can provide a range of benefits for both physical and mental well-being. By following these tips, you can start to incorporate natural healing practices into your daily life and improve your overall health and well-being.

Conclusion:

In conclusion, The Natural Healing Handbook is an essential guide that provides effective remedies for common ailments. The book's approach is based on natural healing methods, which can significantly improve a person's health and wellbeing without the need for conventional medicine. The guide offers a wealth of information on natural remedies, including herbs, supplements, and other natural products that can be used to treat various health conditions.

One of the essential aspects of the book is that it emphasizes the importance of taking responsibility for one's health. The guide encourages readers to adopt a holistic approach to health and wellness, which involves considering all aspects of their lives, including their diet, exercise routine, and mental wellbeing. The book's approach is empowering, as it puts the reader in control of their health and provides them with the knowledge they need to make informed decisions.

It is also worth noting that The Natural Healing Handbook is not a replacement for conventional medicine. While natural remedies can be effective in treating many health conditions, there may be instances where medical intervention is necessary. It is crucial to consult with a healthcare provider before trying any new treatment, especially if you have a pre-existing medical condition or are taking prescription medication.

Moreover, the book does not claim to provide 100% guaranteed results. While the remedies outlined in the book have been shown to be effective for many people, individual results may vary. It is also essential to note that natural healing methods may take longer to work than conventional medicine, and they may require a more significant commitment to lifestyle changes.

Despite these caveats, The Natural Healing Handbook is a valuable resource for anyone looking to take control of their health and wellbeing. The guide provides detailed information on a wide range of natural remedies, including their benefits and potential side effects. The book is easy to read and is accessible to anyone, regardless of their level of knowledge or experience.

In conclusion, I would like to thank you for taking the time to read this book and for considering natural healing methods as part of your health and wellness journey. While medicine has its place in the treatment of various ailments, natural remedies can be a safe and effective alternative for many people. I hope that this guide has been helpful to you and that you will continue to explore natural healing methods as part of your ongoing commitment to health and wellbeing. Good luck, and be well!

Made in United States
Cleveland, OH
18 April 2026

35946262R00069